POJK
Purposely Obliterated Jammu Kashmir

By

Namrata Chowdhary

A Book on Geo-Political Region of POJK & Gilgit-Baltistan

Published by Walnut Publication

#172, K8, Kalinga Nagar

Bhubaneswar - 751003, India

www.walnutpublication.com

ISBN: 9789389355109

Price ₹249

First Published in July 2019

DEDICATED TO THE GREAT PEOPLE
OF
JAMMU & KASHMIR
WHO LIVED TOGETHER PEACEFULLY
IN THE MOST DIVERSE AND RUGGED REGION OF
THE INDIAN SUB-CONTINENT
BEFORE 1947.

AUTHOR'S BIO

Namrata Chowdhary is an Alumni of prestigious St. John College, Agra and University of Jammu. She holds a Masters in Geography from University of Jammu. She has gained a vast experience in subject of Human Geography of Jammu and Kashmir and has acquired in-depth knowledge about the subject. She belongs to the state of Jammu and Kashmir. Currently She is working as Asst. Professor in Geography in Jammu and Kashmir, Higher Education Department.

PREFACE

Jammu and Kashmir are a disputed territory between India, Pakistan and China. The dispute spans from Geographical realm to battle of Ideological supremacy. The state of Jammu Kashmir has witnessed five conflicts since 1947 namely India-Pakistan in 1947-48, 1965, 1971 and 1999 and Indo-China in 1962. What was once a glorious state of Jammu and Kashmir is fighting a continuous degradation since 1947. The different parties to the conflict present the modified and twisted narrative to their population which suits their historical justifications.

The situation in Jammu and Kashmir highlights the important aspect of understanding the basic cause of problem before making an effort to solve the same. Over last 75 years different leaders and Scholars had burned their fingers while trying to solve the issue of Jammu and Kashmir.

This book is written to highlight a completely different aspect of the actual problem of Jammu and Kashmir state and how it manifested to the current situation. The 'Great Game' of the British Empire of having a buffer state between India and the expanding Soviets is known to all. However, the shrewd policies of achieving the dominance of a particular ethnicity over the complete state of Jammu and Kashmir state has been cleverly hidden from the people of Jammu and Kashmir. The Tribal invasion of 1947, the conditions for accession to India and the demarcation of Cease Fire Line achieved a particular set of Geographical and Ethnic divide that completely changed the politics and demographic pattern of Jammu and Kashmir.

This book further makes an endeavor to understand the actual impact of demarcation of Cease Fire line and where the state of Jammu and Kashmir was cleverly steered over the last 75 years. Also, this book aims to bring out the true leaders of Jammu and Kashmir, who mattered the most in 1947 including Sheikh Mohammad Abdullah, Choudhary Ghulam Abbas and Mirwaiz Yusuf Shah, Pandit Prem Nath Dogra, Mahashey Ram Chand and Ahmed Yar Khan 'Duggar'.

History has always exemplified that the main battle in power is over 'Land' and the wish to control the same. The battle for land also becomes murkier when the struggle includes the urge for Ethnic and Religious dominance. Jammu and Kashmir, being a pluralistic and Multi-ethnic land, became a never-ending dispute between the battle of Ethnic and Religious ideologies between India and Pakistan or in more primitive terms Kashmiris and Non-Kashmiris.

ACKNOWLEDGEMENTS

The last two years which I have spent writing this book, many colleagues have generously shared their knowledge and special insights. Chief among these are Prof Sunita Sudan, Dr. Ashaq Choudhary, Dr Mohammad Ashfaq Khan, Dr RP Sharma, Dr Rajni Sharma, Dr Nasir Bhat, Dr Sinduja Gupta, Dr Namita Singh, Mr Ranjot Singh, Mr SK Dhar, Mr Balwan Singh, Mr Majid Malik, Dr. Sukhdeep Sasan and Dr Arun Mahajan.

I also want to acknowledge some source books which were of great help to me in concluding this book: -

Frederic Drew, Jammu and Kashmir Territories

Walter R. Lawrence, The valley of Kashmir

Sheikh Mohammad Abdullah, Autobiography, The Balzing Chinar

Lt Gen SK Sinha, PVSM(Retd), "Operation Rescue"- Military Operations in J&K 1947-49

Lt Gen YM Bammi, Kargil 1999, The Impregnable Conquered

These books are of great importance to understand Geo-political situation of Jammu and Kashmir in 1940s and are very valuable. Without these source books, it would have been difficult to complete my book in correct perspective. These books helped to visualize the past and present position of Jammu and Kashmir in the particular aspect.

Namrata Chowdhary

Contents

LIST OF MAPS Page

CHAPTER 1: INTRODUCTION

This book is written with a purpose to provide a clear and unique image of Jammu & Kashmir state since 1930s. This book will be highly useful to Politicians, peace keepers, Civil Societies, Students and Research scholars and also to Defense Analysts and Policy makers.

The content of this book is deliberately polemical and no doubt that may upset some traditional ideological settings and understandings on the concept and existence of Jammu and Kashmir state. But hope that it will provide a different vision to the state of Jammu and Kashmir and may help to solve its political problem persisting since 1930s.

The State of Jammu & Kashmir lies between Latitudes 32°30′ to 36°N and Longitude 73°30 to 80°E. It included not only Jammu & Kashmir but Ladakh, Baltistan & Gilgit areas also. It had a total area of 68000 square kilometers in 1930s.

The chapter two of this book deals with the ethnic spectrum of Jammu and Kashmir. It will give a brief account of various ethnic communities living in the State. Although the main focus is on Chabhali region or Chabhali Ethnic community living in POJK and Indian Jammu & Kashmir. Finally, this chapter deals about the four Muslims Ethnic ghettos of Jammu & Kashmir state in 1930s.

The chapter three deals with Gilgit-Baltistan province and the treaty of 1935 and impact on Jammu & Kashmir State. The importance of Gilgit-Baltistan was well understood by the British Empire, which always calculated it as a "Buffer" in the 'Great Game' against the Soviets. However, the demographic layout of the region holds a significant dimension to the overall state of Jammu and Kashmir but never being factored till date.

The Chapter four is about the ideology of Pakistan's origin and the impact of this ideology on Jammu and Kashmir State. How Sheikh Mohammad Abdullah rose to became one of the most charismatic leaders and how rift developed between Abdullah and Choudhary Ghulam Abbas of Jammu and Kashmir Muslim Conference over the issue of relative representation in general council of Jammu & Kashmir.

The chapter five attempt to explain how Kashmiri ethnic group were a minority in a state according to census review of 1940s as compared to other groups. The Jammu and Kashmir state once viewed in totality with regards to ethnic and demographic distribution will highlight the importance and dominance between various groups.

Chapter six deals with the concept of East Jammu (Dwigrath Desh) and West Jammu (Lahanda). While the East Jammu were Hindu dominated population and west Jammu had Muslim dominated population. In one of the great ironies of the history, both these regions were divided in 1947 between India and Pakistan. The question is whether the division was a fate of history or a very well thought plan to achieve a greater design.

Chapter seven deals primarily with the tribal invasion of 1947's in Jammu and Kashmir. It further throws light on how Indian Army planned for the various operations to deal with invaders. It attempts to explain how LOC is drawn to keep the West Jammu – to keep the west Jammu (Chabhali region) out of state as a result of which Kashmir valley became power center in the next few years. The astonishingly indistinguishable alignment of LOC and the boundary of East and West Jammu cannot be just a fate of history but rather something more.

Chapter Eight tries to give a retrospective review of ideologies of Sheikh Mohammad Abdullah and Choudhary Ghulam Abbas Khan. The differences of approach and ideology led to a power struggle between the towering personalities and ultimately led a dominance battle between the both. While Sheikh Mohammad Abdullah wanted Jammu and Kashmir as an independent state, Choudhary Ghulam Abbas was in favor of joining the state of Pakistan.

Chapter Nine is a reflection on the tug of war between the Sheikh Mohammad Abdullah and Ghulam Abbas Khan over the two-nation theory about the formation of India and Pakistan based on the Communal lines. It shows that how negative ethnocentrism leads to political obliteration of the state.

Chapter Ten deals with the question that how religious ethnicity can be used to gain power or authority. The demographic and ethnic distribution of Jammu and Kashmir State made it an ideal region to be manipulated on religious and ethnic lines. Both the leaders, Sheikh Mohammad Abdullah and Choudhary Ghulam Abbas tried to mobilize the masses on the basis of religion and ethnicity. This led to state of Jammu and Kashmir into a never ending ethnic and ideological conflict which remains unresolved even today.

Chapter eleven gives a brief account of ethnic and demographic genocide of 1947 and no court of Inquiry was established to investigate it's causes and aftermath. The victim of power struggle between Maharaja, Sheikh Mohammad Abdullah and Choudhary Ghulam Abbas were common people of Jammu and Kashmir. The major violence and damage were witnessed by people of Jammu and Gilgit Baltistan.

Chapter twelve deals with the concept of 'Nirdiyai Dharti' and why this land can never be at peace. The creation of Pakistan and the dispute over the state of Jammu and Kashmir is a classic example of an ideological conflict turning into a conflict of Geography. The demographic divide created on the two side of currently divided state of Jammu and Kashmir will be hard to bridge in near timeframe.

Chapter thirteen explains the plight of Jammu-Sialkot railway line and the apathy of the government towards it. The culture and historic link to Sialkot - once a thriving transport link - has been systematically erased from the physical realm over a period of time.

Chapter fourteen deals with the cycle of violence that civilians living along the International Border /Working boundary faces with the defense forces personnel on both sides in POJK and Indian Jammu and Kashmir.

Chapter fifteen is an actually a philosophical question that whole world is it? And periphery areas of Jammu and Kashmir belong to which world.

I have done my best to bring information regarding Jammu and Kashmir up to date. With this, hope that this book will prove to be useful for the welfare of people of this country, I wish good luck and happy reading.

GEGRAPHICALLY, WHERE WE ARE?

ETHNICALLY, WHO WE ARE?

CHAPTER 2: ETHNIC SPECTRUM OF JAMMU & KASHMIR STATE

Ethnicity in Jammu & Kashmir State

Ethnicity in simple words, is a sense of belonging ness. It defines individuals who are believed to share common characteristics that differentiate them from the other collectivities in a society. An ethnic group is a collection of people which can be distinguished on the basis of: -

(a) Unique cultural traits - Language, Cloths, Jewelry, religion etc.

(b) A sense of Community (membership by Birth).

(c) Territoriality or tendency to occupy a distinct geographical area.

The basic purpose of an individual to take refuge in a particular ethnic group may be *Self Protection* at many times.

In Jammu & Kashmir state, we find ethnic pluralism. Ethnic pluralism is the co-existence of a variety of distinct ethnic groups within one society. Ethnicity or Ethnic belonging to a particular Geographical place has played an important role during First & Second World War. It has also played an important role in context of the state of Jammu & Kashmir.

"Ethnic Pluralism is one of the important characteristics of J&K. The following is the list of races which has a distinct geographical distribution and such characteristics as to render the description & separation of them practical[1]."

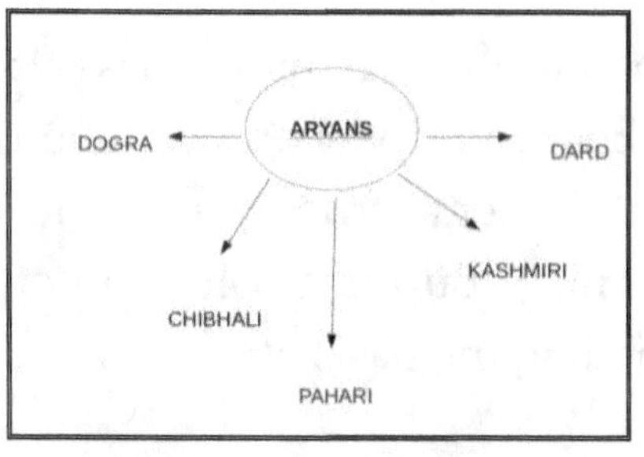

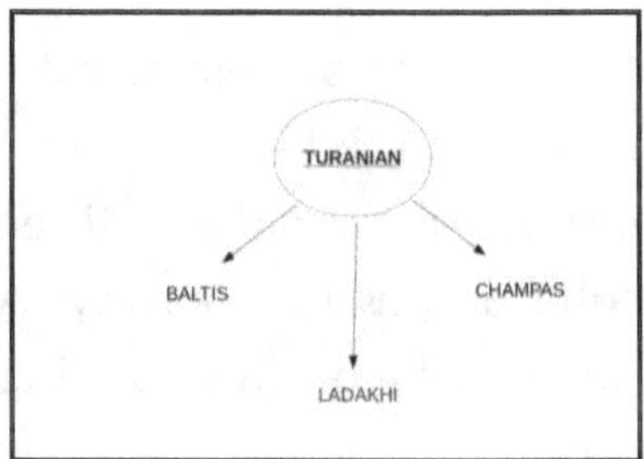

These can be illustrated as following as all these carries different characteristics.

Inhabitants of the Outer Hills

The Dogra Ethnic Community - The Dogras are of the great Aryan race that settled in and has become the main population of India; those of that race who spread into the mountain, or rather , who settled in the lower hills and went into the region whose snowfalls, acquired in the long course of centuries, characteristics that distinguish them from the inhabitants of the plains on the one hand, and of the higher mountains on the other.

The settlers in the hills edge the Punjab, at all events those of them who have retained their Hindu faith, bear, the name Dogra, while the Country they inhibit called is called

1 Drew, Frederic, 2009, Jammu and Kashmir territories. Srinagar, Kashmir Gulshan Publications (Pg.- 6)

Dugar[2]. The name has been derived from the two lakes of Mansar and Surinsar, which means "the country of two hollows" and that's why the land is called Dugar.

They are further divided into various castes as in the Hindu System as

Brahmin.
Rajput- Main and working Class.
Khatri.
Thakar.
Jat.
Dhiyar.
Megh.
Dum etc.

At present, they are largely Hindu ethnic community, concentrated in the region between Tawi & Chenab rivers of Jammu & Kashmir.

The Chibhali Ethnic Community: - They are so called from the name of their country, Chibhali, which is that part of the outer hill region lying between Chenab & Jhelum River. Chibhalis are Muhammadans now but they were in fact of the same race as the Dogra Hindus.

According to Frederic Drew 1875- several tribes of these Muhammadans have the same name as certain of the castes

---

2 Drew, Frederic, 2009, Jammu and Kashmir territories. Srinagar, Kashmir Gulshan Publications (Pg. 33-34).

of the Dugar. Thus, Some of the subdivisions of the Hindu Rajputs, as Chib, Jaral. Pal etc, exists also among the Muhammadans; and the general designation of Mussalman Rajput was commonly used[3].

In Simple terms we can say that the region lying to the west of the Chinab saw the conversion to Islam of the Rajput Clans. This happened largely as the Rajput Population in Jammu is thickest around the Mughal road leading from the plains of Western Punjab into Kashmir through the Bimber-Rajuri-Shupian route across the Pir Panjal. Besides Rajput, there were many Muslim Jats in the Chibhal area. The Jat in Chibhal area were very much similar to cultivating caste in the Punjab; although their numbers were few.

In Eastern part of Chibhal are Muhammadan Thakars. They are found mainly in Reasi, Rajouri, Udhampur and Kishtwar districts of Indian Jammu and Kashmir. The Chibhalis are Hindu Dogra Rajput's converted to Islam and were very much stronger, more muscular than the other and were quite active.

In the pre independence period, The Muslim Rajput population was more than double that of the Hindu Rajput's. The Chibhali area is a home to many different clans including: -

Jatts.

Mangral Rajputs.

---

3 Drew, Frederic, 2009, Jammu and Kashmir territories. Srinagar, Kashmir Gulshan Publications (Pg.- 43) Chibhal – Wikipedia

Gujjars.
Gakhar Clans.
Sudhans.
Sikhs.
Tarkhans.

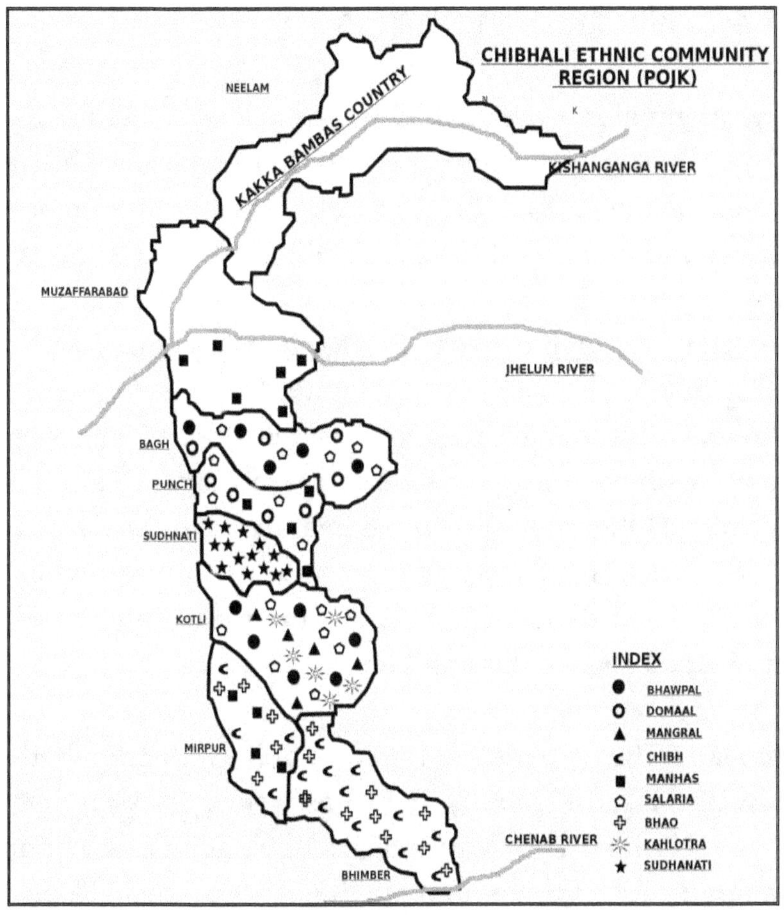

At Present context, Chabhali or Pahari Rajput's, mainly found in the Mirpur-Kotli-Rajouri-Poonch region, now bisected by the Line of Control and Akhnur, Mendhar, Haveli, Riasi and Noushera on Indian Jammu and Kashmir.

This region is located in the Pir Panjal range. These mountains form part of the Inner Himalayan region, run from East-Southeast to West-Northwest across the Indian state of Himachal Pradesh and the disputed territories comprising of Indian Administered Jammu & Kashmir and Pakistan administered Azad Kashmir, where the elevation varies from 1400 m to 4100 m (13500 ft).

"The mountains are traversed by the rivers Chenab & Ravi, with Chenab also forming a cultural boundary, with tribes located in the east of the Chenab remaining Hindu, while those found in the west have generally converted to Islam[4]".

Important chibhali tribes of POJK/Azad Kashmir/J&K

Bhawpal or sometime pronounced as Bhopal, are Rajput Clan within the Chibhali community. In Azad Kashmir/POJK, they are found mainly in Kotli district & Bagh District, in Villages near the Line of Control, while in Indian Administered Jammu & Kashmir, they are found in Rajouri, Naushera & Jammu Tehsils.

Domaal: - They are mainly found in Poonch district (both in J & K and Azad Kashmir/ POJK) as well as in Bagh district of Azad Kashmir and Rajouri district of Jammu & Kashmir.
Mangral: - Also Pronounced as Mahngral, Mangar. They are closely associated with the history of the town of Kotli which was said to be founded by their ancestor Raja Mangar Pal.

---

4 https://en.m.wikipedia.org/wiki/Chibhal.

Mangral rule over kotli state lasted for approximately four centuries until they are defeated by the army of Sikh leader Ranjit Singh. The Mangral led by Raja Shah Sawar khan initially defeated the Sikh forces in two battles (1812 & 1814), though at a very high cost in loss of life. However, The Sikh army returned in 1815 with 30,000 soldiers and a final battle ensued. Having lost many fighters, the Mangrals agreed to a compromise, giving up control of their city (Kotli) to Ranjit Singh.

The rural areas remained under the control of various mangral families as jagris from the Jammu Raj, and they continued to be the landowners & collectors of the tax revenues. This arrangement lasted until Pakistan's 1962 land Reform act, where by the ownership of the land was transferred to the tenant farmers without compensation to the landowner.

Chib: - Also pronounced as Chibh, are found in Bhimber. The Chib have given their name to Chibhal region lying between the Jhelum & Chenab rivers; and on the southern edges of the Pir Panjal region. This is because the Chib ruled of Bhimber effectively covered the territory that the latter became known as chibhal.

There are in essence Dogras who have converted to Islam. The Chib trace desent from Partab Chand, a katoch Rajput prince of Kangra, who said to have ended Thakial rule in Mirpur Bhimber region and established the Chib dynasty.

Minhas: - In terms of distribution, the Dogras Manhas are found Punch Jageer, and the adjoining areas of Muzaffarabad & Mirpur. These Minhas had strong connections with those in Rawalpindi & Jhelum.

Sulehria: - In Azad Kashmir/POJK, Salaria are found mainly in Kotli, Bagh & Poonch districts, while in Indian Jammu & Kashmir Salaria inhabited districts include Rajouri & Poonch.

Bhao: - It means 'Fear' in the local Dogri language. The bulk of the Muslim Bhao population was founded in Bhimber and Hindu Bhao in Akhnoor, the region of Jammu bordering Bhimber.

Kahlotra: - They belong to Naushera & Rajouri tehsils of former Reasi districts till 1947, with a smaller number found in the South eastern portions of Kotli Districts. The Muslim Kahlotra also played an important role in the Adam Malia (Nonpayment of Land Tax) & Quit Kashmir movement.

In 1947, at the partition of India, entire Muslim branch of the Kahlotra tribe migrated from the Jammu region to Azad Kashmir/POJK and Pakistan. But they continued use of the Dogri Language.
Other Chabhali clans/races are Sau/Sao, Maliks, Sudans, Gakkars etc were also can be founded in these areas.

Sudan prevails between Poonch & the Jhelum river, maliks in Dahral valley, Gakhars in Kotli and Mirpur.

On the wholes chibhali ethnic community were strong defenders against powerful enemies and long sustained their independence in the hills. They are very much influenced by the Punjabi culture because of their nearest neighbors[5].

Kakka Bamba Ethnic Community: - In the extreme north west of Chibhal, near the borders of Kashmir lives the two races: Kakka & Bambas. They inhabited the banks of Jhelum between Ginghal and Muzafarabad, and up the lower part of the kishanganga valley/ Neelam river. This was called as kakka-Bamba Country.

They were stout & strong built fellows and surly by nature. They occupy intermediate land between Chibhalis & Kashmir's[6].

Pahari Ethnic community: - Pir Panjal region is called as the land of Pahari people in Jammu & Kashmir. 'Pahari' is name given by Dogras who are their neighbors, which in dogri means "Mountaineers" or people living on mountains.
The Pahari ethnic community covers various castes, races, creed, sects and religions. They are Hindus, Muslims & Sikhs but bounded with each other due to cultural affinity & mother tongue "Pahari".
The main areas of Pahari ethnic community are north of Basoli, Ramnagar, erstwhile Riasi, Rajoui, Budhil and then

---

5 Chibhal – New Pak historian: https://newpakhistorian.worldpress.com posted on July 1, 2014 by Newpakhistory.

6 Drew, Frederic, 2009, Jammu and Kashmir territories. Srinagar, Kashmir Gulshan Publications (Pg.- 43).

towards Muzaffarabad. It also includes Bhadarwah, kishtwar. In other words, they are the dwellers on the middle mountains. Low population areas. Culturally, they are a mixture of Dogras & Kashmiris in the areas, while people on Basoli, Ramnagar, Riasi speak Dogri and related languages while in Bhadarwah, kishtwar they speak Kashmiri and have very much Kashmiri culture influence.

The town of Bhaderwah is also known as 'chota Kashmir or little Kashmir' because of presence of numbers of Kashmiri people here. Outside the town lives the local Bhaderwahi population.

Most men in this area wear light grey woolen cloth and a waistband or kamarband- a woolen sort of rope, a short coat and a lui (Looee or blanket). Most of them are Hindu on Southern part & Kashmiri on the North with no clear distinction. The most prominent Hindu caste in this area is Thakar, which usually practice agriculture[7].

Important tribal people in this area are: -

Gaddis: -In the South East of middle mountains (Pir panjal mountains) lives the race called Gaddis (or Guddoes). They are very much associated with chamba area of Himachal Pradesh.

---

7 Drew, Frederic, 2009, Jammu and Kashmir territories. Srinagar, Kashmir Gulshan Publications (Pg.- 70-71).

They are Hindus & belong to several castes but they do not keep their caste rules so strictly. They possess large flocks of sheep & herds of goats and they migrate from one place to another according to the season.

The Gaddi shephard mainly spend their winter in the low hills of the shiwalik range. When snow melts and the high passes were clear they moved on the higher mountain meadows[8].

Gujars: - This is another race found in the middle mountains (Pir Panjal) and outer hills(shivaliks) as well as in plains. The Gujars have their home below in plains & hills. They practice trans-humane but they only summer visitors to the mountains.

Sometimes they occupy a village by themselves; sometimes they share it with others: even in that case: they remain a very distinct body. The Gujjars, socialize within their own fold and not with other Muslims. They are all Sunni Muslims.

Those living in the middle mountains dress in Kurta Pajama and Lui or blanket but those who are sellted around Kashmir adopt dress like Kashmiri people. The Gujars living in Kashmir speaks Kashmiri and those living in the middle mountains speaks Punjabi, Dogri and Pahari[9].

---

8 Drew, Frederic, 2009, Jammu and Kashmir territories. Srinagar, Kashmir Gulshan Publications (Pg.- 69, 76-77).

9 Drew, Frederic, 2009, Jammu and Kashmir territories. Srinagar, Kashmir Gulshan Publications (Pg.- 77).

Kashmiri Ethnic community:- According to Frederic Drew, " The Kashmiri people are doubtless physically the finest of all the races that inhibit the territories of Jammu & Kashmir we are dealing with and I have not much hesitation saying that in size and in feature they are the finest race in the whole continent of India.

Their physique, their characteristics, and their language are so marked as to produce a nationality different from all around, as distinct from their neighbors as their country is geographically separated. They speak Kashmiri language, which is very difficult to understand. The Kashmiris on the other hand are good linguists. They understand Punjabi or Hindustani also.

Kashmiri ethnic community has more variety in the inhabitants than other part of the Jammu & Kashmir. These are as follows: -

Kashmiri Hindus:- It is a generally accepted fact that up to about the beginning of the 14th century that the population of the valley was Hindu, and that about the middle and end of the century the mass of the people were converted to Islam, through the efforts of Shah-i-Hamadan and his followers and the violent bigotry and persecution of king Sikander the Iconoclast(W. Lawrence)
The only Kashmiri Hindus left are Brahmans. The Brahmans of Kashmir, are known as *pandits.* Besides there are few khattris, Sikh brahmans are also found in the Kashmir ethnic community.

Kashmiri Muslims: - The Kashmiri Muslims are mostly engaged in agriculture in rural areas, while in Srinagar city they work as shawl weavers, or handicraft work like papier - Mache, painting, woodworks, or silver work. They are descendants of the original Hindus, who are converted to Islam.

The main division among them are

Shekhs: - They are converted Hindus and they do not marry into families of menials and market gardeners.

Saiyads: - They fellow 'Pir' profession (pir muridi) and agriculture. They as pir looked upon with high esteem. 'Mir' is the 'Kram' name of the saiyads when they do religious services.

Mughals: - They came to Kashmir during Mughal times and are few in number. Their krams are Mir (a short form of Mirza), Beg, Bandi, Bach & Ashaye.

Pathans: - They speak pastu(in extreme North) and Kashmiri and were found in uttar Machipura tehsil (Handwara). The machhipura Pathan belong to the Yusufzai Section and are known as Marufkhani pathans. They pathans are given the title of Khan, who trade with Peshawar.

Bombas: - The Bombas are believed to have immigrated in Kashmir from Turkey and they are mostly found in Machipura Tehsil (Handwara Tehsil) and they take wives from the Hatmal & Kahka families of the country below

Baramula. The Heads of Bomba families are addressed as Raja and the tract in which they live is known as Rajwara.

Faqirs: - There are several villages of Faqirs or professional Beggars. They work as agriculturalist during the summer season & beg during the winter season. They regard begging as honorable profession[10].

Other tribes in valley of Kashmir with low social status: -

Dums	-	**Village Watchmen**
Galawans	-	**Horse Keepers**
Chaupans	-	**Shepherds**
Band	-	**Profession of singing & acting**
Hanjis	-	**The boatman of Kashmir**
Watals	-	**The gypsies of Kashmir**

Dards or Dardistan Ethnic Community: - The Dards are an Aryan race. A race found along the Gilgit river (Gilgit & Astore region). They are very different and easily distinguishable from Kashmiris. They inhabit the highly mountainous country North of Kishan Ganga river and valley of Kashmir. It includes the Gilgit valley, the Astor Valley, the Dras Valley and some spots along the Indus valley. There are certain subdivisions of the Dard race which may be called castes. The following are the important caste divisions in order of their recognized rank.

Ronu (Ruling Class) – keep some offices of power.

---

10 Lawrence R. Walter, 2005, The Valley of Kashmir, New Delhi, Asian Educational Services. Pg. 302-318.

Shin- (Religious sect of the Dards). There is a peculiarity of manners most strange and curious attaching to this Shin caste of Dards. The thing is this: They hold cow in abhorrence. They look on it in much the same way that the ordinary Muhammadan regards a pig. They will not drink cow's milk, or do they eat or make butter from it. Nor even will they burn cow dung, the fuel that is so commonly used in the East.

Yashkum- they do agriculture.

Kremin- They act as potters, millers, Carriers etc.

Dum- They are treated as unfit for social interaction or menial clan.

There are two divisions among the Dards

Muslim Dards: - It is not enough to say that these dards are Muslims; they are divided into three separate Muslim sects – Sunni, shia & Molai.

Sunni & Shia require no description, as the division exists in almost every part of the Muslim world. The Molai sect corresponds very nearly, or it may be exactly, with that sect called Nur Baksh which we found in Baltistan, which was a modification of the Shia. The name must have it origin from the Arabic Maula, God, they thus calling themselves "the Godly". In matters of prayers and fasting, they follow the Sunni way but in creed (as regards the proper succession of

Muhammadan's successors of the Khalifat) they are Shias. The Molais and Shias will drink wine, the Sunnis will not.

Buddhists Dards: - Along the Indus valley in the "Central Ladakh" are some villages inhabited by Dards who follows the Buddhist faith. They follow Lamas as spiritual leaders. They belong to shin caste because all those customs concerning the cow, which saw to be characteristics of that caste, are held by these Buddhist Dard to the extreme degree[11].

Balti or Balti ethnic community

The country itself is by the Ladakhi's called Baltis, and a native of it is called Balti pa; but the Kashmiris and other neighbors use the word as an adjective, and call the country, according to the Persian form, Baltistan, or the place of the Baltis.

Baltis are Mohammedanised Tibetans. They are quite the same stock as the Ladakhis, differing from most of the latter in physical character little more than some Ladakhis differ from others. In other words, they are Ladakhis converted to Islam.

In adopting Muhammadanism, the Baltis dropped the customs of polyandry and have since to some extent polygamy. The result is that Baltistan is crowded; The population is overflowing.

---

11 Drew, Frederic, 2009, Jammu and Kashmir Territories. Srinagar, Kashmir, Gulshan Books Pg. 248-249, Pg. 295-299.

It is curious thing that Baltis belong mostly to the Shia sect of Muslims. A number of the Baltis call themselves "Nur Baksh" (spiritual leader).
Baltistan is one of the homes of Polo. This is so thoroughly the national game of the Baltis that almost every village has its polo ground, enclosed and carefully kept for the purpose.

Baltis Ethnic community occupy, either partly or wholly, the valley of certain tributaries of the Indus & considerable length of shayok valley and of the Indus valley itself, down to 6000 feet above the mean sea level[12].

Ladakhis Ethnic Community: - Beside Indus & Shyok Valley, they occupy the whole of Zanskar, and they made a small settlement on the both sides of the snowy range. The Ladakhis are cheerful, willing and good tempered, they are ready for a laugh and they are not quarrelsome. The men wear a 'choga' (a wide long coat) and the women a 'gown' (A skirt). The ethnic community follow Buddhism as religion. Like baltis they are also of Tibetan race. The Ladakhi is also called Bodhi.

The Ladakhis have formed villages and have occupied nearly all the ground fit for cultivation who still retain the Buddhist faith which is held by the Tibetans to the South East and East[13].

---

12 Drew, Frederic, 2009, Jammu and Kashmir Territories. Srinagar, Kashmir, Gulshan Books Pg. 248-250.

13 Drew, Frederic, 2009, Jammu and Kashmir Territories. Srinagar, Kashmir, Gulshan Books Pg. 168.

Champas ethnic community: - The champas are nomards, occupying the tract called Rupshu, in the South Eastern portion of the country, as far as it is inhabitable; their tents are pitched in the high-level valley at elevation varying from 13,700 feet; below this they do not come.

They also belong to Buddhist faith/religion. They are most hardy and a most cheerful set of people, living all their lives in a severely cold climate and getting a scanty subsistence, they still have the best of the spirits[14].

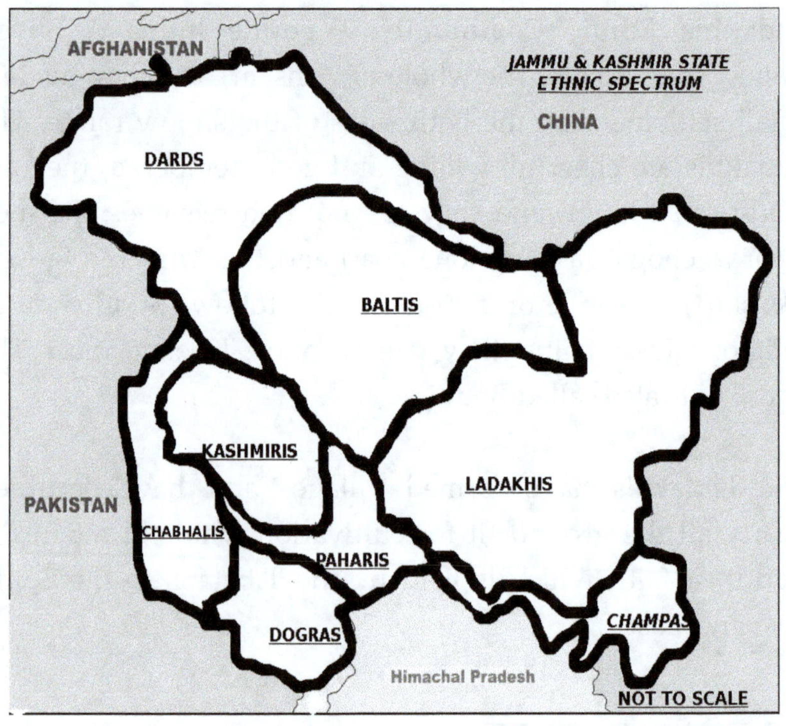

14 Drew, Frederic, 2009, Jammu and Kashmir Territories. Srinagar, Kashmir, Gulshan Books Pg. 169.

<u>Four Muslims ethnic ghettos in 1930s in Jammu & Kashmir include</u>: -

Baltis – Baltistan

Dards – Dardistan

Kashmiris- Kashmir valley

Chibhalis - **Pakistan** occupied Jammu and Kashmir

These are the four ethnic Muslim Ghettos of 1930's having some common features but they are also differing in some different ways like history, language, food, cloth, culture and lifestyle. In order to be power center, one ethnic ghetto has to sub-duct the other. The Baltis and Dards had low population as compared to Chibhalis and Kashmiris.

In the later period, the Kashmiri ethic community was able to dominate the politics because by the act of 1935 between Britishers and Maharajas, Gilgit- Baltistan province was under British Political agent. Therefore, Baltis and Dards were cut off from the mainland (Jammu and Kashmir). And Chibhalis Region was also got dissected from Jammu and Kashmir by the Tribal invasion of 1947-49, Kashmir political parties become prominent in the state.

The Kashmiri ethnic Ghettos would not have got prominence in the state as other three groups are difficult to control both geographically as well as politically and culturally if they remained the part of the Jammu and Kashmir State.

Consequently, after their exclusion from the state, the Kashmir Valley became the 'Pivotal center' of politics in Jammu and Kashmir.

CHAPTER 3: GILGIT-BALTISTAN PROVINCE

(Its importance and the treaty of 1935)

The year 1935 also saw an important event in Jammu and Kashmir state. It was the agreement between the British Government & the Maharaja Government over Gilgit's administration.

The special interest that the British Government took in Kashmir was due to its border touching Russia from the Gilgit-Baltistan province. After the Bolshevik revolution in Russia, the British Government got more alert and their interest got diverted towards Gilgit-Baltistan area of the Ladakh wazarat & the hill states of Hunza Nagar. And it was handed over to the British Government for lease for 60 years by Maharaja of Jammu & Kashmir giving proof of his loyalty. And also, in the 1930s, it was proving to be difficult for Maharaja to govern the Gilgit wazarat under the local rule of Kashmir government[15].

in 1935, the British government leased the Gilgit-Wazarat from Jammu & Kashmir and it came under the direct administration of the political agent. In terms of the agreement, the Maharaja had abdicated his military and civil responsibilities and thus the region fell directly under the British rule for a period of sixty years.

---

15 Abdullah, Sheikh Mohammad, 2013 The Blazing Chinar- an Autobiography, Srinagar, Kashmir P 160-163.

Lord Curzon underlined the importance of Gilgit to India (British India) in the following words; "It is one of the Northern gates of India through which an invader must advance, if it advances at all. Gilgit occupies a strategic place and the Indian Government, harassed by Russia's growing restlessness in Central Asia, knew it for the Key of great Northern gateway into India, A key North holding even at some cost in toil, money and valuable human lives".

It has a total area of 72, 971 km^2, which is six times of Azad Kashmir/POJK. Major languages include Balti, Shina, Burushaski. The Population in Gilgit perceived itself to be ethnically different from Kashmiris & disliked being ruled by the Kashmir state. This area was divided into three parts which can be illustrated as following:

1. **Gilgit Astore**- This district comprises the Gilgit-Wazarat with its own governor (Wazir-e-Wazarat).

2. Gilgit Agency- It includes

(a) Chilas states or Diamer districts.

(b) Ghizer districts or punial, yasin, Kuh-Ghizar & Ishkoman.

(c) The Hunza and Nagar state, is governed by political agent or British Indian Government.

3. The **Baltistan or Little Tibet** includes: - Ghanche, Shigar, kharmarg, Skardu[16].

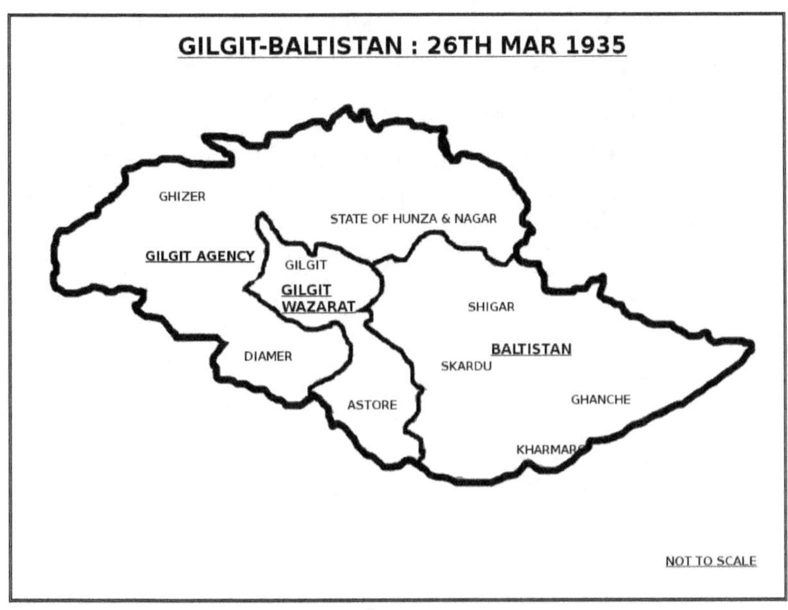

Prior to 1947, Baltistan was part of the princely state of Jammu & Kashmir. Baltistan and Ladakh were administrated jointly under one wazarat(district) of the state. Skardu tehsil as main tehsil & leh and kargil as other districts.

The people of Gilgit Baltistan opposed any integration with Kashmir and instead want Pakistani citizenship and constitution status for their region. In fact, the people of the region were in favor of joining Pakistan and this part is also inaccessible from Azad Kashmir/ POJK.

16 Drew, Frederic, 2009, Jammu and Kashmir Territories. Srinagar, Kashmir, Gulshan Books Pg. 169.

Toni Morrison "Playing in the Dark!"

Silence from and about the subject was the order of the day. Some of the silences were broken, and some were maintained by authors
who lived with and within the policing strategies
What I am interested in are the strategies for breaking it[17].

17 Drew, Frederic, 2009, Jammu and Kashmir Territories. Srinagar, Kashmir, Gulshan Books Pg. 169.

CHAPTER 4: IDEOLOGY OF PAKISTAN & JAMMU AND KASHMIR STATE

The Muslim resurgence in India started with the Aligarh movement, the purpose of which was to rehabilitate, through western education, the economic and social status of Muslims, with a view to ultimate political emancipation. Aligarh Muslim University and other Muslim education institutions were established and the All India Muslim League founded in 1906.

The idea of separate Muslim state was first put forward by poet-politician Allama Iqbal (a famous and distinguished poet from Kashmir belonging to a Brahmin Pandit Sapru clan, whose family had converted to Islam a generation earlier), in his address to the All India Muslim League at Allahabad in 1930. He talked of a "Muslim Homeland to be formed in the North West of India" but within a united India. Later, at the time of the Round table conferences in 1930-32 in London, Choudhary Rahmet Ali a post graduate student at Emmanuel college, Cambridge, urged the Muslim delegates to abandon the idea of a federal government of a combined India, and instead press for a separate homeland for Muslims, for which he coined the name Pakistan. The literal meaning of Pakistan being "Land of the Pure[18]".

---

18 Bammi, YM (Lt Gen) (2002), kargil 1999, The Impregnable Conquered, New Delhi, Natraj Publishers Pg. 23.

The Acronym of Pakistan include

P- Punjab
A - Afghani
Ki - Kashmir
S - Sindh
istan - Baluchistan

In 1940, the All India Muslim League, meeting of Lahore, under the president ship of Quaid-i-Azam, Mohammad Ali Jinnah, adopted what is popularity known as "The Pakistan Resolution".

This advocated independent state of Muslims in the Muslin Majority blocks in the West & East of India.

Seeing the British mood giving representations to Muslims in 1944 Choudhary Rehmat Ali advocated ten separate "Nations" with in the continent of "All-Dinia", including the oceanic dependencies. His pamphlet "Millat & Her Ten Nations", issued on June 10, 1944 and re-issued on March 12, 1946, envisaged combining nations of Siddiqistan, Faruqistan, Haideristan, Ministan, Safistan, Nasaristan, Bangistan, Osaminstan, Pakistan, Mapalistan.

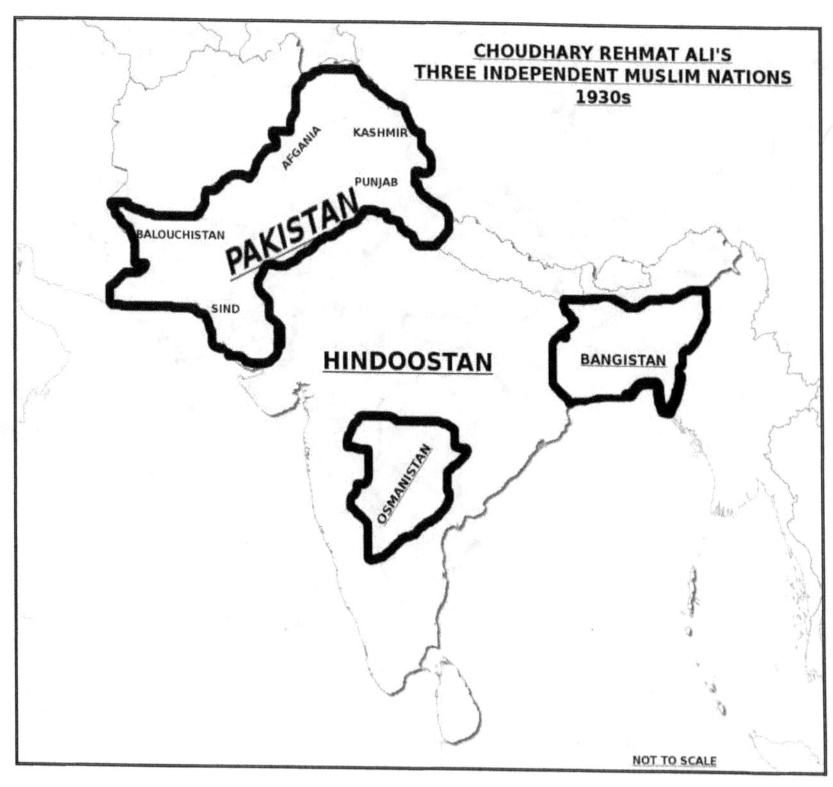
CHOUDHARY REHMAT ALI'S
THREE INDEPENDENT MUSLIM NATIONS
1930s
KASHMIR
AFGANIA
PUNJAB
BALOUCHISTAN
PAKISTAN
SIND
HINDOOSTAN
BANGISTAN
OSMANISTAN
NOT TO SCALE

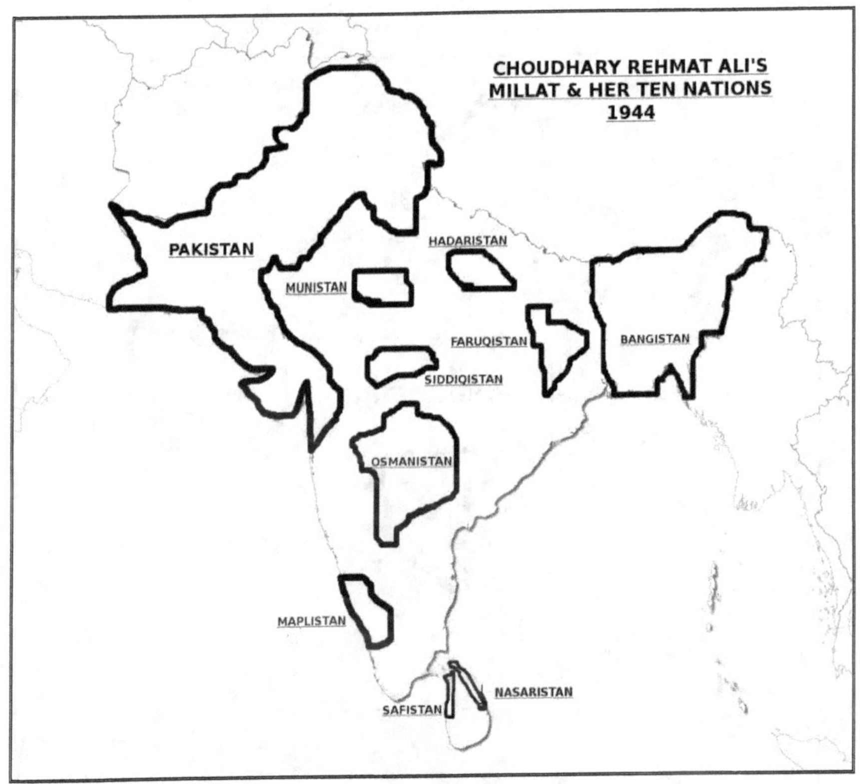

The Indian National Congress was alarmed that the acceptance of two Nation theory may credence to Ten Nation claim. But Jinnah adopted a rigid & uncompromising stance with the Congress and insisted on the partition of India on religious and communal Lines.

Ultimately, in that same year (1946), a British Cabinet Mission arrived in India and after discussions with political leaders, put forward a plan for the transfer of power.

The Scheme proposed three autonomous zones of provinces in United India; a western zone including N.W.F.P, the Punjab, Sind & Baluchistan; an eastern zone including

Bengal & Assam and a middle Zone comprising the rest of India.

And after Negotiations between Indian National Congress and the Muslim League, British made the declaration on 3rd June 1947, partitioning India between Hindus and Muslims. Pakistan emerged on the political map of the world on 14th August 1947 with Karachi, the birth place of the Quaid-i-Azam, as its capital.

The western and eastern wings of the country separated from each other by a distance of 1000 miles, came to be known as West Pakistan & East Pakistan. The West Pakistan consisted of the provinces of the North West frontier (N.W.F.P), Baluchistan, Sind, West Punjab and the Small princely states of Chitral, Dir, Swat, Amb, Kalat, Lasbela, Kharan, Bahawalpur and Khairpur[19].(K.U kureshy, HOD of Geography, University of Punjab, Lahore 1978).

Although Quaid-i-Azam Jinnah got what he wanted but the very idea of Pakistan also included 'K' Kashmir, which is missing from the West Pakistan. That is why Muslims of Pakistan in-spite of having such a large share from India as well as from Jammu & Kashmir remains un-contented.

Quaid-i-Azam Jinnah & Ch. Rehmat Ali's ideology of "Pakistan including Kashmir" was countered by Sheikh Abdullah. Jinnah, though not on good terms with either the

---

19 Kureshy, KU (1978), A Geography of Pakistan, Karachi, Oxford University Press (Pg. 1-3)

Maharaja of Jammu & Kashmir or Sheikh Abdullah was confident of acquiring Kashmir for Pakistan because it was a Muslim majority state.

Addressing students of AMU, Jinnah has professed that "Islam believes in democracy, and we learnt democracy 1300 years ago, and will never cherish anti-democracy forces".

However, when asked by Mirza that we must try to be considerate to Muslim League, as after all they gave us Pakistan, Jinnah retorted haughtily "Who told you the Muslim league gave us Pakistan? I brought Pakistan - with my stenographer". Thus, while in India, it was the will of the people which won Independence, in Pakistan it was the "Chosen elite" who claimed the honors[20].

Jinnah clamoring for recognition made him cold, rigid & uncompromising. Jinnah called 1946 Quit Kashmir agitation as "movement of hoodlums".

Sheikh Mohammad Abdullah: - A charismatic Leader

He was the popular leader of the masses of the Kashmir valley who enjoyed the confidence of Gandhi and Nehru. By 1930's Kashmir Muslims had acquired the image of lazy and uneducated laborer while only few could excel as artist, craftsmen, artisans. It was Sheikh Mohammad Abdullah (Also called **the Lion of Kashmir or Sher-e-Kashmir),** who

---

20 Bammi, YM (Lt Gen) (2002), kargil 1999, The Impregnable Conquered, New Delhi, Natraj Publishers Pg. 32.

reawakened the spirit of Kashmiri and gave them courage to resist the oppressor.

By impacts of his personality and self-sacrifice, he became the force to be reckoned with and was often imprisonment for his anti-establishment acts. He was fascinated by the poetry of Iqbal so much that he recited his revolutionary verses with such feeling that the congealed blood of the hearers would come to a boil. He had also very much inspired by the Karl Max ideology. He wanted to make Kashmir like 'Switzerland' of Europe.

13 JULY 1931, MARTYRS DAY(YOUM-E-SHUHADA-E-KASHMIR)

On 21 June 1931, at the premises of the shrine of Khanqah-e -mualla, Sheikh Mohammad Abdullah recited the poem with this couplet:

> ***Ai khuda de zor -e-dast -o - baazu-e-haider hamein***
> ***Phir ulatana hai saff -e-kufr-o-dar-e-khyber hamein***
> ***God! Grant us the strength of haider***
> ***So, we defeat the infidel troops and enter the gate of Khyber[21].***

And after the speech, he along with other and public took an oath on the holy Quran that they would never waiver in their commitment to nation. Here, he clearly points out the 'battle of Khyber' and also of the 'infidels' troops. What is the meaning of 'infidels' troops '? Why did not he use the king troops or anarchy government. 'Nation' mean Muslims nation or Kashmiri nation! These rationale to these arguments is elaborated in later part of the book.

In 1931, he clearly used religion and the Quran's text for the political purpose. What are political needs of that time?

Muslim in Kashmir were divided into so many sects as Hanafis, Ahle Hadithn, Ahmadiyas, Ahkle Sunnah, Shittes, and Sunnis. Even Hanafis are further divided in Tsecha and kott. Their mutual conflicts have thrown them into total dis-

---

21 Abdullah, Sheikh Mohammad (2103), The Blazing Chinar, Srinagar, Gulshan Books Pg. 75.

tray and Kashmiri Muslims divided. If they were to be united, there should be common platform. The platform is provided by Masjids / Shrines and Dargahs and religious Quranic sermons to ignite people. Sheikh Abdullah knew how to use religion as 'opium of masses' as denoted by Karl Max to unite people. At that time, most of the Muslims of valley are uneducated and living a life of poverty, they perceived Sheikh Mohammad Abdullah as their leader who will save them from the tyranny of Dogra Rule.

Sheikh Abdullah continued to unite people with his rallies. On 12 July 1931, he along with Maulavi Abdur Rahim, Gulam Nabi Gilkar, urged people to ready themselves for the ultimate sacrifice. The speeches went on till midnight, and on 13 July 1931, while the Abdul Qader's case hearing was to take place at central jail, large masses of people gathered around the central jail. The governor, Raizada Trilok Chand ordered the police to open fire. In all, 21 persons were martyred on the occasion.

At many places Muslims stormed shops and plundered them like in Maharaja Ganj area. Maulavi Abdur Rahim, khawaja Ghulam Nabi Gilkar and Sheikh Abdullah was arrested. The three representatives from Jammu who had reached Srinagar a few days before are Chaudhary Ghulam Abbas, Sardar Gowhar Rahman and Yaqub Mistry were also arrested.

The Hindu press, like Milap, Pratap and the Tribune covered the incident as a conflict between Hindu and Muslims or on communal basis while the editors of Inqilab covered the incident as oppression of the Dogra regime.

On 24 july1931, Miyan Afzal Husain convened an All-India conference of Muslims at the residence of Sir Zulfaquar Ali khan, which was attended by many Muslims leaders. Discussions were held on how to extend help to Kashmiri Muslims. As a result, **the Kashmir committee** came into being.

Mirza Bashir -ud -din Mahmood, Khalifa of the Qadiyani community was elected president and Mr. Abdur Rahim Dard Secretary.

The Kashmir committee celebrated 14 Aug 1931 as "the Kashmir day "in India and the state of Jammu and Kashmir on that day. Srinagar observed an unprecedented shutdown.

The Maharaja Government of Jammu and Kashmir appointed Raja Hari kishen koul as prime minister. Koul has sensed that it would be difficult to control the situation without establishing a liaison with the Muslim leaders. He approached Nawab Sir Mehr Ali Shah, the son of Punjab's great spiritual divine Pir Sahib, who had formed an association called the Hizbullah(God's party).

Similarly, Mirza Ghulam Ahmed, Qadiyani leader and the Pir jammat Ali Shah was also invited, but the situation in Kashmir got more worse. All-India Kashmir committee dispatched an elected delegation comprising Mr. Abdul Rahim Dard, Maulana Ismaeel Ghaznavi and Sayyid Habib editor of Siysat. It was proposed that then new organization would be called the **All Jammu and Kashmir Muslim conference**, and was formed in 19th Oct 1932. Sheikh Mohammad Abdullah and Chaudhary Ghulam Abbas along with Mirwaiz Yusuf Shah founded the All Jammu and Kashmir Muslim conference to oppose the Maharaja Hari Singh's rule. In which sheikh Mohammad Abdullah was unanimously elected the first president of the conference. Sheikh Abdul Hamid advocate was nominated as vice president of the party, while Chaudhary Ghulam Abbas and Maulavi Abdur Rahim Vakil were chosen as general secretary and secretary respectively.

Rift between Sheikh Mohd. Abdullah and Chaudhary Ghulam Abbas

On the closing day of the All Jammu and Kashmir Muslim conference, their started a hot debate regarding the relative representation of Jammu and Kashmir. The delegates from Kashmir argued that since Muslims were in the majority in Kashmir, they needed to be given representation in the General Council according to their ratio. But Chaudhary Ghulam Abbas and Allah Rakha Sagar argued that since the Muslims of Jammu province are politically more alert and advanced / informed, they should get more representation. The delegates from Jammu indirectly pointed out the supposed inferiority of Kashmiris at that time. The Punjabi style Muslim Dogra ethnic community (or Chibhali ethnic community) was not able to digest or **tolerate** the Kashmiri leadership as they call them "hatho" - unhygienic and illiterate. '

Hatho was the derisive term for Kashmiri. Sheikh Mohd. Abdullah has written in his book 'The Blazing chinar 'that: "**the Kashmiri delegates, who had come from the far-flung parts of the valley were a pious lot with little knowledge of the way of the world. but the attitude of the people from Jammu was so supercilious and annoying that even they were hurt, their wounded sense of dignity giving them blood - shot eyes".**

Sheikh Mohd Abdullah did not like their attitude. His ego was hurt. He said in an impassioned tone: "**How sad! It is the Kashmiri who have made sacrifices. They have offered their blood for their land and given up on their possession for it. But look at the fence sitting people of Jammu, abusing and mocking us[22]!".**

Here the fence sitting people means the Muslims Dogra ethnic community (or Chibhali ethnic community).

---

22 Abdullah, Sheikh Mohammad (2103), The Blazing Chinar, Srinagar, Gulshan Books Pg. 124-125.

CHAPTER 5: CENSUS ANALYSIS OF JAMMU AND KASHMIR STATE 1940

As per census of 1941, total population of Jammu & Kashmir state was 4021616. The comparative analysis of population of Jammu and Kashmir as per region is depicted below.

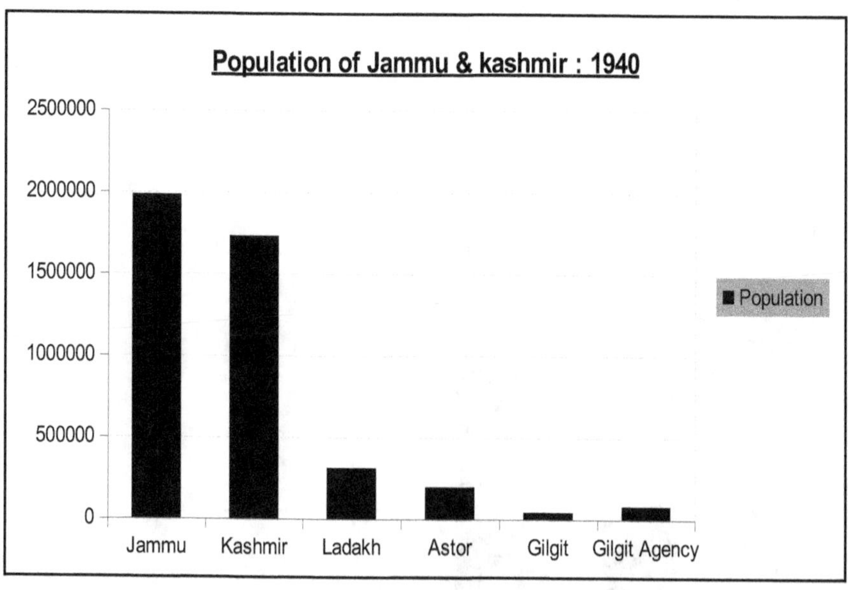

Out of which, the population of Jammu province was 1981433.

Kashmir province had 1728705 persons.

Ladakh had 311478 persons.

Astor had 195431 persons.

Gilgit (leased area) had 39521 persons.

Gilgit Agency had 76526 persons[23].

---

23 Census of India, 1941, Vol XXII, Jammu and Kashmir part I and II.

In 1941, The area of Astore, Gilgit (leased area), Gilgit Agency was under the British Political Agent for 60 years by the treaty of 1935 between Maharaja government and British Indian government.

According to the census of 1941, out of 1981433 persons in Jammu province, the distribution was: -
642110 – Hindus
1215676- Muslims
38566- Sikhs
85081- others

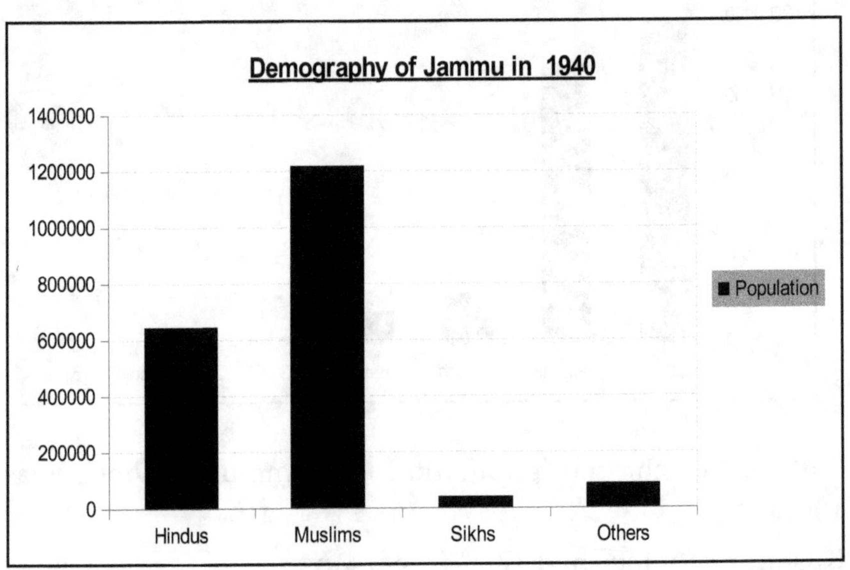

In other words, Muslims constitutes 61.35 percent in 1941 of the total population of Jammu province and were in majority.

On the other side, Kashmir province had 1728705 persons. In other words, Kashmir province had 42.98 percent population out of the total state population.

Out of 1728705 persons of Kashmir province in 1941, 200,000 were Kashmiri Pandits and 27337 were Sikhs. If the population Kashmiri Pandits and Kashmiri Sikhs are taken out, the remaining Kashmiri Muslim population was 1501368 persons.

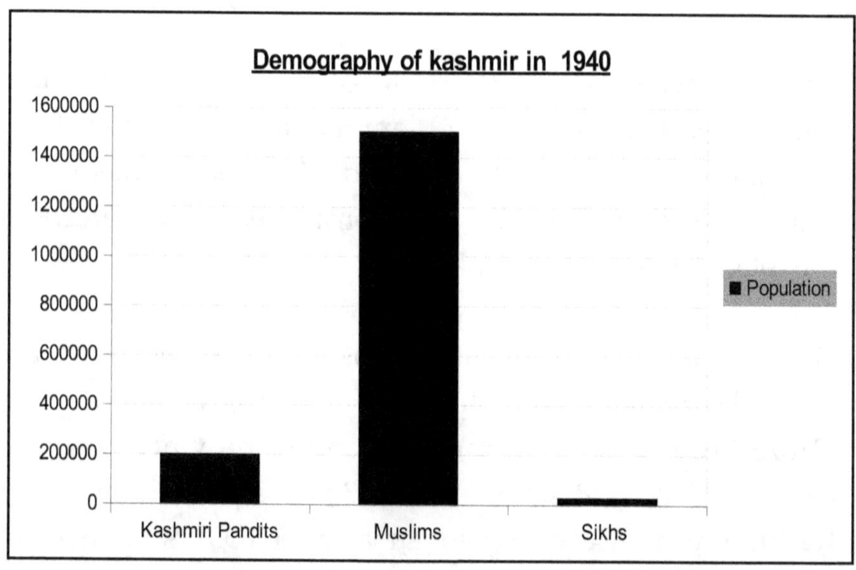

This 15 Lakh approximate Kashmiri Muslims in 1941 constitute 37.3 percent of the state population. Out of this 15 Lakh population, approximately 10 percent living in the periphery of the valley are non-Kashmiri Muslims like Gujars, Bakarwals and Pahari's, who linguistically belong to the family of languages spoken in Jammu and if Shias and other small ethnic pockets for examples Buddhist etc. are taken into account, Kashmiri Muslims were minority in the state in 1941. And Kashmiri Muslim percent will be reduced to 28% of the Jammu & Kashmir state.

On the other hand, if 1215676 Muslims of Jammu province which formed 30.22% of Jammu and Kashmir State population and 272431 Gujars and 14511 Bakarwals of the state were taken together, they constituted 37.36 percent of the total state population of 1941.

Geographically, in terms of area, as per the census report of 1931, the total area of the state was 84471 square miles (218780 square kilometers). The Jammu province occupied an area of 12, 378 square miles (32067 square kilometers), Kashmir province occupied an area of 8539 square miles (22166 square kilometers) and the frontier districts of Gilgit & Ladakh occupied 63, 554 square miles (164604.86 square kilometers)[24].

---

24 Dr Vaid SP, (2009), Socio-economic roots of unrest in Jammu and Kashmir (1931-47), Jammu, Shyama Publications.

Jammu province Area	Kashmir Province Area
12378 sq. miles	8539 sq. miles

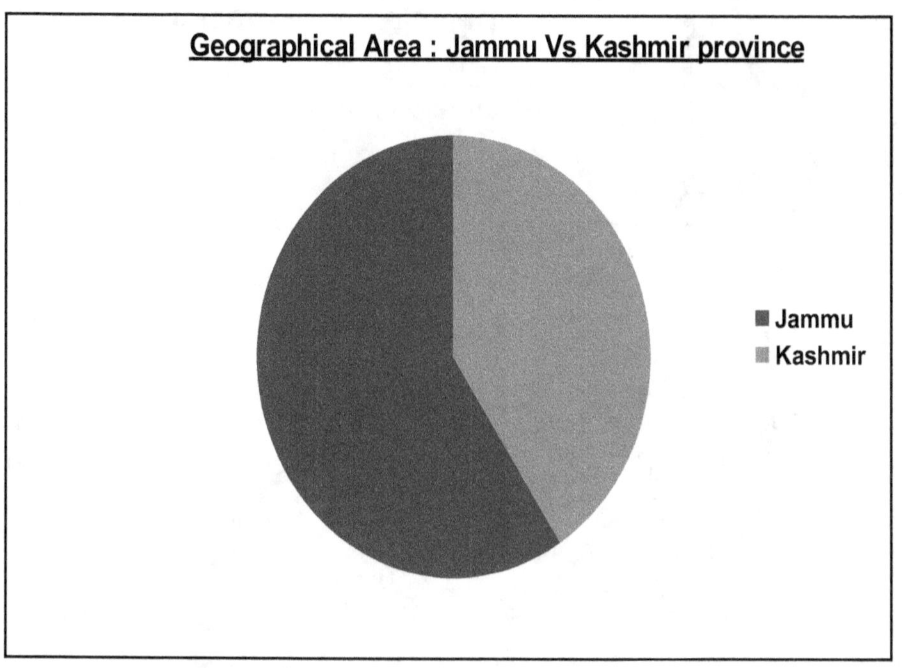

It is clear from the pie diagram; Geographically Jammu province is bigger than Kashmir province.

CHAPTER 6: CONCEPT OF EAST JAMMU & WEST JAMMU

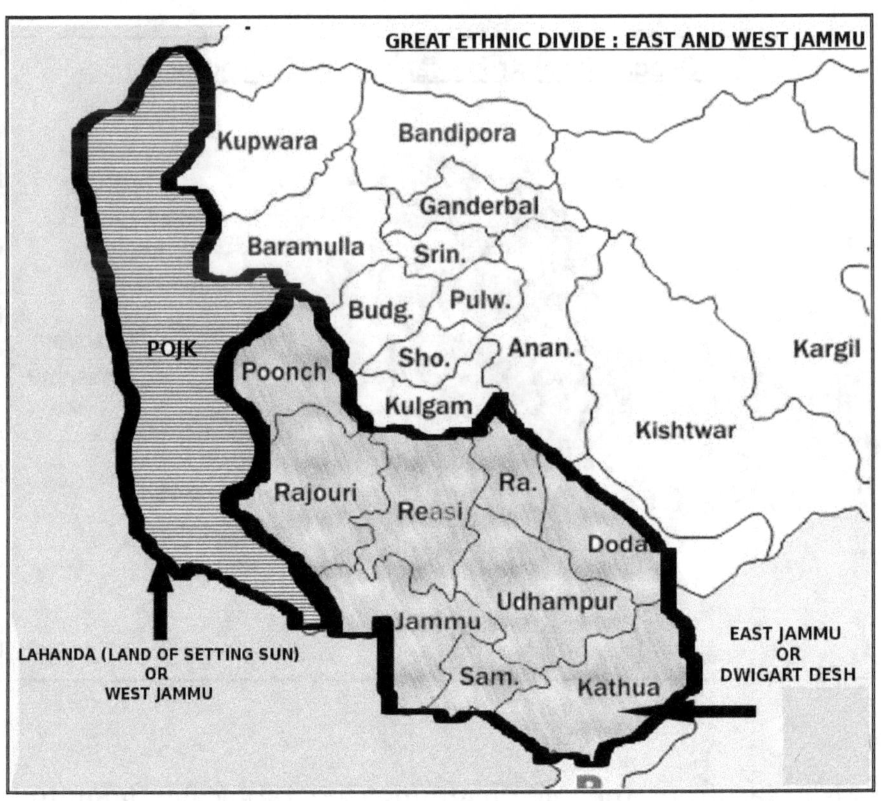

West Jammu

Chibhali Muslims ethnic community as discussed earlier resides in the West Jammu (Lahanda). They had a very good relations with Gujjars (a simple tribal people of migratory lifestyle type). The word Lahanda is a Punjabi language word meaning the "setting sun" or the west. This word "Lahanda "is used as the synonym for the western Dogra chibhali Ethnic Community. The principle dialect of this area is "Lahanda" besides pothawari & poonchi were spoken mainly in Poonch & Mirpur. The Lahenda or the Chabhali land included the part of outer hill region of Jammu & Kashmir between the Chenab & Jhelum rivers. The population of this area in 1940s included Dogra Muslims and few Hindus and Sikh pockets who had close affinity with Punjabi culture. Basically, they are Dogra Hindus converted to Islam. In 1941, it included Muslim Rajput, Jats, Kashmiri Muslims and Sudans.

East Jammu

It included Dogra Hindu ethnic community which speaks Dogri Language. Their main area lies between Ravi and Chenab in Jammu & Kashmir. It includes kathua, Samba, Ramnager, Udhampur, Reasi districts.

The word Dogra is said to have arisen from the fact that the cradle of the Dogra people lies between the two lakes of Surisar and Mansar. Its derivations are therefore from the word Dwigarth Desh (Meaning country of two hollows). Which was converted into Duggar and Dugra which then became Dogra. The term Dogra does not refer to single caste but more a linguistic category. The people in East Jammu includes Brahmin, Rajput-Mian and working class, Khatri, thakar, Jats, Dhiyar, Megh and Dums etc.

In 1940s Kashmiri Ethnic Community sees the Chabhali Muslim ethnic community or fence sitting people as his political rivals. It was very much clear from the census of 1941 that

1. Demography point of view- Kashmiri Muslims are minority.
2. Geographically, the area of Jammu province is more the Kashmir province.
3. Socially, the Chabhali ethnic community is closer to Dogra ethnic community and Gujjars than Kashmiri Muslim ethnic community.
4. Economically, the Chabhali ethnic Muslim community were more prosperous than kashmiri Muslims.
5. Politically, the Chabhali Muslim ethnic community are closer to Punjab (pre-partitioned Punjab) Political Parties of that time such as Qaidaini party.
6. Chibhali Muslim Ethnic Community are closer to Punjabi culture through matrimony and commerce.
7. Railway facilities upto Jammu also help chibhali community to interact with Punjab.
8. Since due to agreement of 1935, Gilgit -Baltistan was under British Political agent.

Keeping in view the above circumstances, it is a clear idea that even if Maharaja government of Jammu & Kashmiris abolished, the Kashmiri Muslim ethnic community or valley will not be the 'power center' which is a minority as per census of 1940s.

CHAPTER 7: TRIBAL INVASION OF JAMMU & KASHMIR 1947

Political Situation in 1947

The future of Kashmir was muddled when the Maharaja dithered in making decision by 15th August whether to join India or Pakistan. Jinnah was bent upon taking Kashmir into Pakistan by all means. Finding the Maharaja Dithering till 15th August 1947, he applied pressure by enforcing an economic blockade of state of the Jammu & Kashmir. The Maharaja sought to placate Pakistan by offering Standstill Agreement, which was accepted by Jinnah but declined by Nehru. Ultimately the Tribal invasion or the Razakars invasion from North West frontier Province provide him the opportunity in 20th Oct 1947. Over 2000 Raiders in motor lorries poured across the borders from Pakistan. These raiders were a motley crowd comprising Hazara tribesmen, Afridi's, Muslim league, National Guard and Pakistan Army personal said to be 'on Leave'. They were equipped with complete range of infantry weapons including machine guns and heavy Mortars. It was obvious that this large force has been assembled, equipped and launched into battle by Pakistan. It was a regular invasion of a peaceful neighboring state without any of the formalities of declaring war[25]. The main Tribal Invaders column advanced along the Domel road heading for Srinagar, their supreme objective. Their advance was swift and was made easier by the desertion of

---

25 Bammi, YM (Lt Gen) (2002), kargil 1999, The Impregnable Conquered, New Delhi, Natraj Publishers Pg. 50-51.

some personal of the state forces guarding the Domel-Abottabad road. An attempt was made to put up resistance at Garhi - 90 Miles west of Srinagar, but in view of the invaders overwhelming numerical superiority, any such attempt was doomed to failure. Garhi fell to the Invaders on the 22nd Oct 1947.

Thereafter, the Invaders developed a three-pronged attack on the communication center of Uri from Uri, Muzaffarabad, Domel and Punch. Yet another attempt was made to stem this advance. Brigadier Rajender Singh of the state force gathered a small force of only 150 men and held out at Uri. He was successful in delaying the enemy for two very precious days but in doing so, this small force was completely annihilated and its gallant commander killed. Having captured Uri, the Invaders entered Mahura on the 24th Oct, where they damaged the power house, plunging the whole of Srinagar into darkness. Therefore, they advance to Baramulla, only 35 miles from Srinagar[26].

It was at this stage on 24th Oct 1947 that Maharaja of Jammu & Kashmir sent an SOS message to Lord Mountbatten, the then Governor General of India. The Maharaja wrote, "with the condition obtaining at present in my state and the great emergency of the situation as it exists, I have no option but to ask for help from the Indian Dominion. Naturally they cannot send the help asked for by me without my state acceding to the dominion of India, I have accordingly

---

26 Lt Gen Sinha, SK (1977), Operation Rescue - Military Operations in Jammu and Kashmir 1947-49, New Delhi, Vision Books private limited Pg. 17-19.

decided to do so and I attached the instrument of accession for acceptance by your government.

The other alternative is to leave my state and my people to freebooters. On this basis no civilized government can exist or be maintained. This alternative I will never allow to happen so long as I am the ruler of the state and I have life to defend my country. I may also inform your excellency's government that it is my intention at once to set up an interim government and ask Sheikh Abdullah to carry the responsibility in the emergency with my prime minister. If my state has to be saved immediate assistance must be available at Srinagar. Mr. Menon is fully aware of the gravity of the situation and he will explain to you if further explanation is needed".

On the 26th Oct 1947, the Maharaja signed Instrument of Accession to the Indian union and on 27th Oct 1947, India sent her forces to fight the raiders in Kashmir and save Srinagar, the people and the state of Jammu and Kashmir. Sheikh Mohammad Abdullah was released from the Jail to take over the administration of Jammu and Kashmir. Indian forces showed great bravery and courage in difficult and rugged terrain and harsh climate of extreme cold in state of Jammu and Kashmir. After Baramulla is recaptured, Srinagar got saved from the raiders.

The Indian Army examined the following plans for the possible operations[27]:-

1. DUCK- Capture of Kargil with a view to link up with Leh. This would also eliminate the threat to the Jammu Srinagar road from the East through Kishtwar.

2. EASY-Link up with Punch from Rajouri and thereby present enemy infiltration from this area towards Riasi and on the Jammu-Srinagar road from the west.

3. CAMEL-Capture of Hajipir pass. This would liquidate the threat to Uri from the south as also afford a link up with Punch.

4. SNOOK- Capture of Bhimber and thereby remove the threat to Naushera from the south.

5. STEEL- capture of Kotli.

6. CRAB – capture of Muzaffarabad.

7. BLOOD- Capture of Mirpur.

The Government had decided that Leh and Punch must be held at all costs. Therefore, the first three operations DUSK, EASY and CAMEL were undertaken, Indian Army successfully covered these three operations. But the last four

---

27 Lt Gen Sinha, SK (1977), Operation Rescue – Military Operations in Jammu and Kashmir 1947-49, New Delhi, Vision Books private limited Pg. 86-87.

operations SNOOK, STEEL, CRAB and BLOOD were not carried out because of Pt Nehru Diplomacy. Pt. Nehru had taken the dispute to United Nations. The cease-fire sponsored by the United Nations came into effect on Jan 1, 1949. This cease fire had been ordered in Kashmir after fifteen months of Hard fighting.

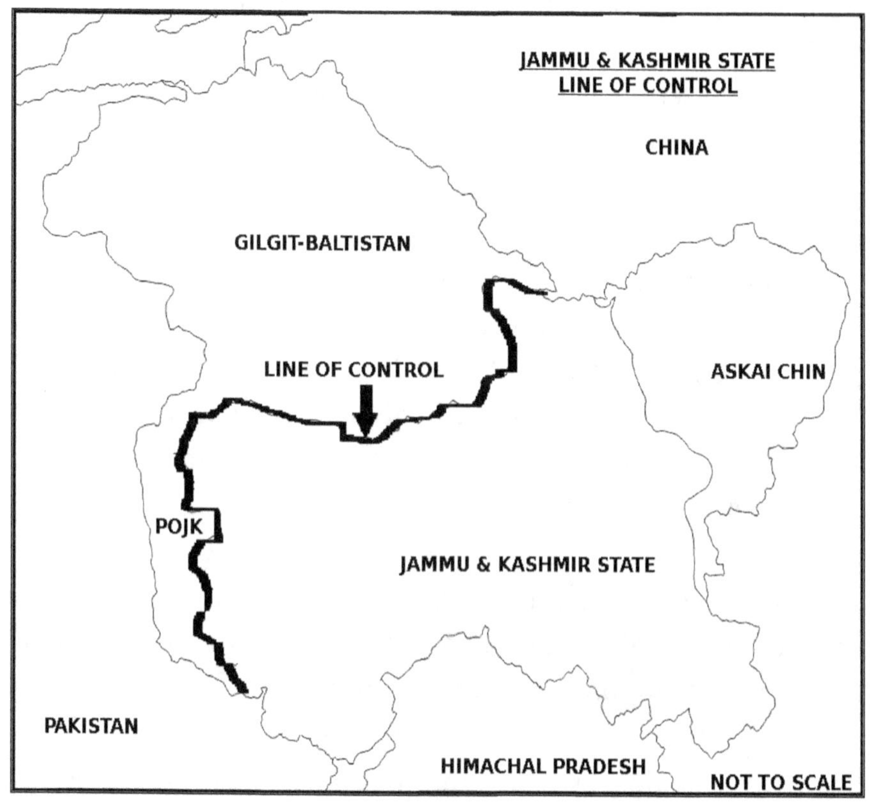

This line of approximately 800 Kms drawn on map cut across low hills, Nullahs, forested mountains and high features in Jammu and one valley region, separating the opposing troops. In Ladakh region, the cease fire line was drawn connecting high peaks on the watershed and it cut across glaciers.

Because of non-operation SNOOK, STEEL, CRAB, BLOOD the areas of Mirpur, Kotli, Bhimber and Muzaffarabad (Lehanda or land of setting sun) went to Pakistan. But if reviewed ethnically, it is the division of Jammu province into two parts - East Jammu and West Jammu.

As discussed earlier, West Jammu (Lahanda) contain Chinhali ethnic community and East Jammu included Dogra Hindu ethnic community.

The people got divided on the communal basis 'very deviously', as like the partition of Bengal was done by the Lord George Nathanial Curzen in 1905. It was a masterpiece of Curzon's internal policy. It divided Bengal in two parts- East Bengal & Assam as Muslim Bengali dominated area and West Bengal as Hindu Bengali Dominated area.

Evidently, it was an attack upon the growing solidarity of Bengali nationalism, an attempt to undermine the traditions, history and language of the Bengalis[28].

The same analogy was repeated in Jammu province. Jammu province was divided into two parts as East Jammu containing Hindu ethnic community and West Jammu (Lehanda) containing Chibhali or Dogra Muslims. Indirectly,

---

28 Groves, BL & Alka Mehta (2010), a New look at Modern Indian History (From 1707 to the Modern times), new Delhi, S.Chand & Company limited Pg. 222.

it was an attack upon the traditions, history and languages of the Dogra Hindus and Chibhali ethnic community. Their culture (society's reservoir of knowledge and thoughts) got demolished beyond recognition.

In other words, it led to subduction of the areal ethnicity. Therefore, Jammu province was politically dismembered which is now referred to a POJK (Pakistan Occupied Jammu & Kashmir), should be called Politically/Purposely obliterated Jammu & Kashmir province. Indirectly, it helped Kashmir based politics.

Why it was done?
FOR PANDIT. NEHRU?????

Directly it satisfied the emotional attachment of Pt. Nehru with the land of Kashmir.
Among Kashmiri Brahmins- whose loyalties drew them towards Hindustan had become important leaders in Indian Politics, and their voices were powerful in the councils of Delhi, Chief of them was Pandit Jawahar Lal Nehru, whose emotions over his native land were described when he said to a British Army Officer, "In the same way that Calais was written on Mary's heart, Kashmir is written on mine".[29]

For Sheikh Abdullah??

---

29 Bolitho, Hector, (1954), Jinnah Creator of Pakistan, Reproduced by Sani H. Panhwar Pg. 163.

1. Because according to 1941 census, Kashmiri Muslims are in minority and Democracy is the government of majority.

2. The Sheikh Abdullah fund it difficult to sell the slogan" Dogra Raj Murdabad" in Jammu.

3. If Chibhali Muslims ethnic community was within Jammu & Kashmir, the Valley cannot be the power center.

4. Kashmiri based politician sees the fence siting people as their political rival as they are more attached to Jinnah & concept of Pakistan and Punjabi Culture.

5. Sheikh Abdullah wanted to replace the Maharaja's rule but cannot work under the Jinnah or Nehru ideology.

AFTERMATH

Before the partition, Jammu was the most populous region of the state. The cease fire line on 1 Jan 1949 was so drawn as to keep the non-Kashmiri Muslims area outside the Indian part of the state as the people in Pakistan administered parts of the state do not speak Kashmiri and belong to the same ethnic stock as Jammu.[30]

---

30 Puri, Balraj, (2010), Chapter 1 Identities, ideologies & Politic. Identity politics in Jammu & Kashmir, edited by Rekha Chowdhary New Delhi, Vistasta Publishing private limited Pg. 33.

On the Whole, and soon afterwards, in the political arena, the center of gravity shifted from Jammu to Srinagar after the formation of popular government in the state.

Formerly, the upper caste Hindus, in general and the Rajput's in particular, were at the helm of affairs of the state but after 1947 the Muslims, especially of the valley, became the new elite in politics and administration. Now, their voice was considered to be the voice of entire state. At the height of Jammu-Kashmir tension, before 1953 Jammu was represented by one minister in the National Conference cabinet of Five. Besides, none of the important office bearers of the party in power i.e. President, vice-president, general secretary and treasurer was from Jammu.[31]

Not only this it became a convention that the chief Minister must invariably belong to the valley as it was essential to appease the Kashmiris.

Previously, Hindus of the state were in favor of the state's full autonomy and many of them in 1947 even wanted to be independent. But now the role was reversed. While the Kashmiri Muslims became the champions of the state's autonomy or self-rule, the Hindus became advocates of closer integration with India.[32]

---

31 Vaid, SP, (2009), Socio-Economic Roots of Unrest in Jammu & Kashmir (1931-47), Jammu, Shyana Publications Pg. 96-97.

32 Vaid, SP, (2009), Socio-Economic Roots of Unrest in Jammu & Kashmir (1931-47), Jammu, Shyana Publications Pg. 96-97.

Year 1947 was the year of India-Pakistan divide. Similarly, 1947-48 was the ethnographic divide of Jammu Province. It can be clearly visualized from the alignment of Cease Fire Line and existence of East and West Jammu that it clearly separates both entities. It cannot be merely a co-incidence and without design.

CHAPTER 8 : A RETROSPECTIVE REVIEW OF IDEOLOGIES OF SHEIKH MOHAMMAD ABDULLAH AND CHOUDHARY GHULAM ABBAS

Sheikh Mohammad Abdullah and Ideology of Pakistan.

WHY SHEIKH ABDULLAH LED NATIONAL CONFERENCE DID NOT JOIN PAKISTAN?

Sir Syed Ahmed khan (1817-1898), AMU (Aligarh Muslim University) and Sheikh Mohammad Abdullah

In 1875, Sir Syed Ahmed laid the basis of Aligarh Muslim University, which in turn produced the scholars and professionals who started the 'Idea of Pakistan' movement. Although Sir Syed Ahmed khan was dedicated to Muslim modernization, Islam's destiny and the idea of Pan Islamic identity. He indirectly motivated a separate state for Indian Muslims but did not mention it during his lifetime. Sheikh Mohammad Abdullah was one of the students of Aligarh Muslim University. He had studied M.Sc. Chemistry from AMU. He was very much influenced by Sir Syed Ahmed Khan and Karl Marx.

Dr Mohd Allama Iqbal and Sheikh Mohd Abdullah

Dr Allama Iqbal in his own way propelled the idea of Pakistan as effectively as Jinnah or Sir Syed Ahmed Khan. He, too began as an advocate of Hindu Muslim unity, and one of his poems "Tarana - e- hind "(Indian Anthem) is still a popular song in India (it begins, "our Hindustan is the best place in the world …").

Later, Iqbal turned the idea of separate homeland for Indian's Muslims into a mass movement, drawing intellectual, professionals and community leaders into the fold. He heightened the community pride - the community being defined as the Muslims of India - and credibly argued that this community desired and needed a separate state in which it could establish a south Asian counterpart of the great Islamic empire of Persia and Arabia. For Iqbal, this state - he did not call it Pakistan - would not only solve India's Hindu Muslims puzzle, it would awaken and recreate Islam, freeing it from both alien Hindustan and obsolescent Islamic encrustations.

Iqbal idea of Pakistan was not based on a European model of nation state, but on "an acute understanding that political power was essential to the higher ends of establishing God's Law[33]".

---

33 Philip Cohen, Stephen, 2004, Washington DC, Brooking's Institution Pg. 25-30.

Thus, Iqbal saw '**Territorial Nationalism'** as a step towards a larger Islamic community, a vehicle for the perfection of Islam.

Jinnah's led Muslim League and Sheikh Mohammad Abdullah

By contrast to Iqbal, Jinnah visualized Pakistan as a "nation" consisting of Indian Muslims. He takes Kashmir as "Izzat "means pride and honor to have Kashmir in Pakistan as most of Pakistanis do.

Jinnah's Pakistan means 'Pakistan identified themselves as culturally Indian, although in opposition to Hindu Indians'. He had vagueness in his ideology of Pakistan and he was not able to make the 'consensus on the kind of state Pakistan was to become[34]'.

Sheikh Mohammad Abdullah does not like this vagueness and he often said that "we Kashmiris are unique" by language and culture[35]. Therefore, Sheikh Abdullah led NC (National Conference) did not join Pakistan state.

Sheikh Mohammad Abdullah & Internal Conflicts

In 1932, Mirwaiz Yusuf Shah along with Sheikh Abdullah and Choudhary Ghulam Abbas founded the All Jammu and

---

34 Philip Cohen, Stephen, 2004, Washington DC, Brooking's Institution Pg. 25-30.

35 Abdullah, Sheikh Mohammad, The Blazing Chinar- an Autobiography, Srinagar, Gulshan Books Pg. 181.

Kashmir Muslim Conference to oppose the Maharaja Hari Singh's rule. However, after a year, conflict occurred between Sheikh Abdullah on one side and Mirwaiz Yusuf Shah, Choudhary Ghulam Abbas on the other. In order to expand the group, Abdullah wanted to allow people of other religion to join it. This was opposed by Mirwaiz Yusuf Shah who felt he was "betraying the cause of the Muslims".

Consequently, Abdullah founded the **Jammu and Kashmir National Conference**. However, the Muslims of Jammu and Kashmir felt that it was representative body of the Indian National Congress. As a result, under the leadership of Yusuf Shah along with Choudhary Ghulam Abbas khan, Muslim conference entered into an alliance with the All India Muslim League. And in July 1947, the party passed a resolution demanding the accession of the state of Jammu and Kashmir to Pakistan based on "Geographic, Economic, Linguistic, Cultural and Religious conditions[36]".

The Mirwaiz clan has always being viewed as pro Pakistan? 'No' says Umer Farooq Hurriyat Conference leader. "Rather pro people", my father would always say "He had to face Allah". This fear was always with him[37]. Thus, it is cleared that in July 1947 most of the Jammu and Kashmir people wanted to join Pakistan but it will lead to total destruction of

---

36 Mirwaiz Mohammad Yousuf Shah, Hindustan Time, Retrieved (21 Jun 2017).

37 Sharma, shiv Chander, 2005, Those Who shaped the Destiny of Jammu and Kashmir, Jammu Yak Publishing Channel Pg. 117.

Sheikh Mohammad Abdullah's political carrier. Thus, Sheikh Mohammad Abdullah and its political substances can be viewed as follows.

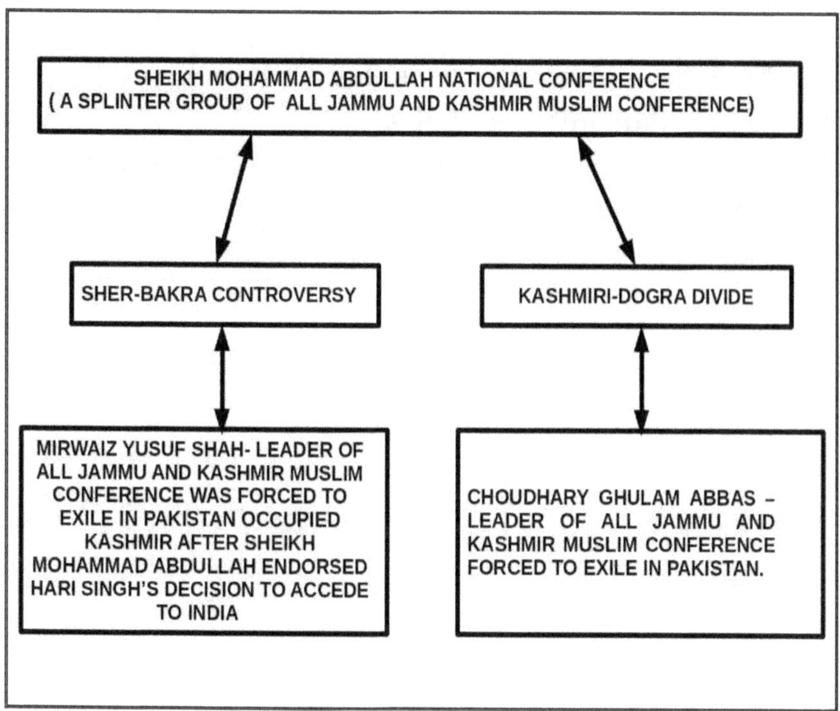

It can be analyzed from the above at that time the position of Sheikh Mohammad Abdullah and its political carrier needed a strong backup and that help is provided by Pandit Nehru and tribal invasion of Pakistan. Therefore, he sided with Pandit Nehru and decided to back the Maharaja in the process of acceding to India over Pakistan after being convinced by the conditions bargained by Pandit Nehru with the Maharaja.

<u>Position of Sheikh Mohd Abdullah</u>

My situation then was somewhat like that reflected in this verse:

"Zahid -e - tangnazar ne mujhe kafir jana.
The devout dub me an infidel
Aur kafir yeh samajate hai ki musalman hun mein
And the unbelieving considers me a Muslim[38]".

Choudhary Ghulam Abbas and Ideology of Pakistan

---

38 Abdullah, Sheikh Mohammad, The Blazing Chinar- an Autobiography, Srinagar, Gulshan Books Pg. 184.

Chowdhary Ghulam Abbas (1904-1967)

Chowdhary Ghulam Abbas was a leading politician of Jammu province and the president of Muslim Conference party. When the state of Jammu and Kashmir was under the atrocities of Dogra Raj and the Muslim majority was being subjugated, Choudhary Ghulam Abbas rose the occasion with great valor and devotion and dedicated his life for the liberation of the people of Jammu and Kashmir.

Earlier life and carrier

Chowdhary Ghulam Abbas was born in the middle-class Gujjar family of Choudhary Nawab khan on 04 Feb 1904 at Jammu. He was graduated from Prince of Wales College, Jammu. He received his law degree from the Lahore Law college and started his carrier as a lawyer in Jammu. He was offered a position of Sub Judge but he refused to serve the Dogra Raj. He won admiration among the Muslim masses by his political ideology. He reorganized the social political organization **"Young Men Muslim Association"** which was established earlier in 1909 and was the only platform that Muslim were using to raise their political voice in Jammu & Kashmir. This organization conducted some massive demonstration against the Dogra rule and its activities[39].

In order to safeguard the rights of the Muslims of Jammu and Kashmir, another organization, All Jammu and Kashmir

39 Choudhary Ghulam Abbas, 19 Dec 2014, Retrieved from Https://www.nation.com.pk/Lahore

Muslim Conference was established. Its president was Sheikh Mohammad Abdullah while Choudhary Ghulam Abbas was elected as its Secretary General.

Later this organization was renamed as Jammu and Kashmir National Conference but Sheikh Abdullah developed his association with Pandit Nehru and the All India National Congress. Choudhary Ghulam Abbas withdrew from the National Conference. As the struggle between the Congress and the Muslim League over the partition of India had its repercussions in Kashmir and the idea of Pakistan gain ground, the National Conference lost its popularity. Consequently, Muslim Conference was revived under the leadership of Choudhary Ghulam Abbas and Aga Shaukat Ali. The Muslim Conference demanded **Kashmir affiliation to Pakistan on 19 July 1947.**

Chowdhary Ghulam Abbas enthusiastically campaigned for the affiliation of people of Jammu and Kashmir with Pakistan. He arrived in Pakistan after the transfer of prisoners in 1948, when the cease fire in the Kashmir conflict took effect. He served the Azad Kashmir government till 1951. He presented the case of Pakistan in the United Nations along with Mohammad Ibrahim Khan when India took the Kashmir issue to United Nations Organization, which ended up with the Cease Fire Line[40].

In 1951 Chowdhary Ghulam Abbas resigned from the leadership of Azad Kashmir Government and set aside from

---

40 Choudhary Ghulam Abbas, 01 Jan 2007, Retrieved from https://www.storyofpakistan.com/Choudharyghulamabbas

m politics. He died of stomach cancer on Dec 18, 1967. and was buried at Faizabad, Rawalpindi, as he willed to be buried in Pakistan.

In 1995 Pakistan postal service issued a commemorative postage stamp to honor his services[41] .

Chowdhary Ghulam Abbas was among the first few leaders who raised then voice of Kashmir's affiliation with Pakistan. He was imprisoned for campaigning the cause of Jammu and Kashmir affiliation with Pakistan. He was symbol of hope for the Jammu & Kashmir's Muslim as he vehemently decreed the Dogra rule in Jammu and Kashmir.

It was often said that Sheikh Abdullah was feared by his charismatic personality. Sheikh Abdullah once said about Chowdhary Ghulam Abbas that "Agar **mera khadd bada naah hota toh Chowdhary Ghulam Abbass mujhe nighal jata" (if my height / status was not big Chowdhary Ghulam Abass would have eaten me up).**

41 Choudhary Ghulam Abbas, 01 Jan 2007, Retrieved from https://www.amazingpakistan.com/Choudharyghulam abbas

CHAPTER 9 : TUG OF WAR BETWEEN SHEIKH MOHAMMAD ABDULLAH AND CHOUDHARY GHULAM ABBAS

Ideological Conflict Between Sheikh Mohammad Abdullah And Choudhary Ghulam Abbas Khan

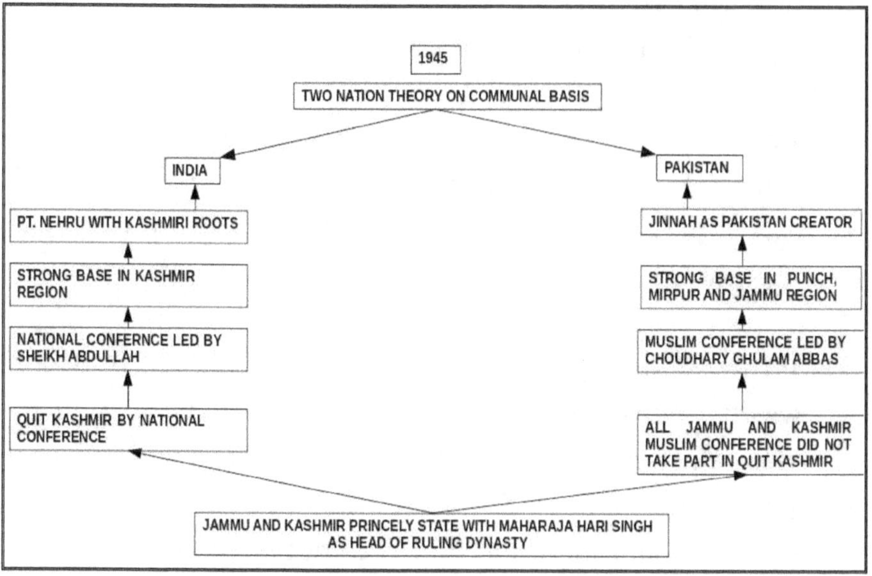

Sheikh Abdullah as a National Conference head had a strong control over Kashmir region. He was very much influenced by the Congress and the Pandit Jawaharlal Nehru, Both Sheikh Abdullah's and Pt Nehru has strong Kashmiri roots.

Sheikh Abdullah, an AMU scholar and a New leader for his political aspiration aligned to Nehru and Congress because he understood very much that political power in Jammu and Kashmir cannot be held without their help as he had no political background like Mirwaiz's in Kashmir. But he was a very kind hearted person from a humble background. He was of liberal nature and great love for Kashmir.

He started to became as secular as he can in his political outlook and established National Conference on the principle of pluralism. Ideologically, he was true follower of Dr. Mohammad Allam Iqbal (a poet and politician) and his concept of Territorial Nationalism.

Choudhary Ghulam Abbas khan, as a leader of Muslim Conference had strong base over Punch, Mirpur and Jammu. He was very much influenced by the Indian Muslim League and the Mohammad Ali Jinnah.

Choudhary Ghulam Abbas as a Muslim Conference leader knows that Muslims people population of state wanted to join the Pakistan as like the Muslims of others states. He has no special interest in Kashmir ethnicity and culture. He sees himself as Muslim first. But that does not mean that he was a fundamentalists or rationalist. Initially, he did not like the principle of plurality of Sheikh Mohammad Abdullah of NC (National Conference) because he feared that in the name of Islam, other Muslim parties inimical to Jammu and Kashmir Muslim Conference can utilize the situation for their own vested interest because it will create confusion among Muslims themselves whose literacy rate are very poor and are not very secular in their outlook . He believed in Jinnah concept of Pakistan that Muslims needed a homeland for their protection and to fulfill the cultural and civilization destiny.

It is clear from the above flowchart that when 'Two Nation Theory' was proposed on communal basis, the Jammu and Kashmir politicians in 1945 were divided into two parts. Choudhary Ghulam Abbas led Jammu Kashmir Muslim Conference wanted to join Pakistan and Sheikh Mohammad Abdullah led National Conference joined India, although wanted autonomy instead of alignment. Consequently, a tug of war started between Sheikh Mohammad Abdullah and Choudhary Ghulam Abbas. While the Sheikh led National Conference started 'Quit Kashmir' movement, Choudhary Ghulam Abbas led Muslim Conference did not take part in it and called it 'Movement of Hoodlums'.

Ideological similarity Between Sheikh Mohammad Abdullah and Choudhary Ghulam Abbas khan

Both of them used religion as a tool for their vested interests. They both knew that religious ethnicity decides the political power bases. The Jammu and Kashmir state had approximately 80:20 ratio of Muslims and Hindus respectively at that time. Religion according to Karl Max "Opiate of the masses". "People become complacent because they have been taught to believe in an afterlife in which they will be rewarded for their suffering and misery in this life. Although these religious teaching soothe the masses distress any relief is illusory. Religion unites people under a false consciousness" that they share common interest with members of the dominant class (Roberts, 2004)[42].

---

42 Kendall, Diana (2007), Sociology in our / times: The Essentials, Sixth Edition, Canada, Thomson Wadsworth Pg. 370.

During 1930's in Jammu and Kashmir, Muslims masses are taught that if they work hard for a religious goal, they would be rewarded richly in another life. Religious text is used for proving this and start 'jihad' against infidels.
(Sura IV vers 74 and 75).

"Let those fight in their cause of God who sell the life of the world for the hereafter, to him who fight in the cause of god – whether he is slain or get victory – soon shall one give him a reward of great (value)[43].

Both Sheikh Mohammad Abdullah and Choudhary Ghulam Abbas khan utilized religion to unite Muslims community in Jammu and Kashmir state against autocratic rule of Maharaja.

But "From a conflict perspective, Religion tends to promote conflicts between groups and societies. According to conflicts theories, conflicts may be between religious groups, or within a religious group, or between a religious group and the larger society. Conflict theories assert that in attempting to provide meaning and purpose in life while at the same time promoting the status quo, religion is used by the dominant classes to impose their own control over society and its resources[44]"

---

43 The Punjab Disturbances Court of Inquiry (1954), Lahore, Punjab, Pakistan pg. 192.

44 Kendall, Diana (2007), Sociology in our Times: The Essentials, Sixth Edition, Canada, Thomson Wadsworth Pg. 370.

(M c Gurie, 2002).

In Jammu and Kashmir, during 1930′ s, the dominant Muslims religious class tried to control over the society and the resources. And when the conflicts started first time, it was within the religious group, i.e. between Dogra Muslims ethnic community and Kashmir Muslim ethnic Community.

While the Gilgit-Baltistan was out of Jammu and Kashmir state politics in 1935 as the British government leased the Gilgit Wazarat from Jammu and Kashmir.

Dogra Muslim Ethnic Community or Chibhalis Ethnic Community	**Kashmir Muslim Ethnic Community**
Choudhary Ghulam Abbas khan	Sheikh Mohd Abdullah

Thereafter, the survival in the politics was seen as who will dominate the scenes of the Jammu and Kashmir in 1947 -48 after Pakistan tribal invasion. And the ethnic religious community which will dominate the political landscape would have control over society and its resources.

Both of them are suffering from Ethnocentrism

"When observing people from others culture, many of us use our culture as the yardstick by which we judge their behavior.

Sociologist refers to this approach as Ethnocentrism-the practice of judging all cultures by one 's own culture" (summer 1959/1906)

Ethnocentrism is based on the assumption that one's own way of life is superior to all others. For example, most school children are taught that their own school and country are the best. The school song, the pledge to the flag, and the national anthem are forms of positive Ethnocentrism. However negative Ethnocentrism can also result from constant emphasis on the superiority of one's own group or nation[45].

While 1930's Jammu and Kashmir, Muslims of Jammu region feels themselves superior to Kashmiri Muslims politically, economically as well as socially. Punjabi style Dogra Muslim ethnic community leader like Choudhary Ghulam Abbas khan, were also an ethnocentric personality while Sheikh Abdullah was very much hurt by this Ethnocentrism because Kashmiris were treated at that time as 'Hatho' -a derogatory work for unhygienic and illiterate person. And Sheikh perceived that Kashmiris had scarified more than the fence sitting people of Jammu division to gain democratic government from Maharaja. According to Sheikh Mohammad Abdullah, "We Kashmiris are unique" by culture and language[46] .So it is clear from the above that there existed a Negative Ethnocentrism between two

---

45 Kendall, Diana (2007), Sociology in our /times: The Essentials, Sixth Edition, Canada, Thomson Wadsworth Pg. 59.

46 Abdullah, Sheikh Mohammad, The Blazing Chinar- an Autobiography, Srinagar, Gulshan Books Pg. 181.

community at that time. And a tug of war was going on simultaneously between two groups over the control of Jammu and Kashmir state after the abolishment of Maharaja's government which is inevitable due to wave of independence in Indian Subcontinent.

CHAPTER 10: RELIGIOUS ETHNICITY AS POLITICAL POWER BASE

Religious Ethnicity as Political Power base

What is Power? According to Max Weber power is "the ability of person or groups to achieve their goal despite opposition from other."
What is authority? "Authority is the legitimate power which one person or a group holds and exercises over another. The element of legitimacy is vital to the notion of authority and is the main means by which authority is distinguished from the more general concept of power. Power can be exerted by the use of force or violence. Authority, by contrast depends on the acceptance by subordinates of the right of those above them to give them orders or directives[47 48]."

The types of political authority were first defined by the Max Weber in his essay "politics as a vocation." In this essay he emphasized that the political authority that controlled the state can be composed of the following types of authority or what is called in German, Herrschaff [3].

Traditional Authority - power legitimated by respect for long established cultural patterns, e.g. Maharaja of Jammu

---

47 Anthony Giddens, Sociology, London, Polity Press 1997 Pg. 581.

48 Max Weber in "Weber's Rationalism & Modern Society: New Translations for the 21st Century" Edited by Tony Water and Dagmar Water Pg. 137-138.

and Kashmir before 1947, Mirwaiz Yusuf Shah of Kashmir etc.

Charismatic Authority: - power legitimated by extraordinary personal abilities that inspire devotion and obedience e g Sheikh Mohammad Abdullah, Choudhary Ghulam Abbas khan.

Rational legal Authority: - Also known as bureaucratic authority, is when power is legitimized by legally enacted rules and regulations such as governments.

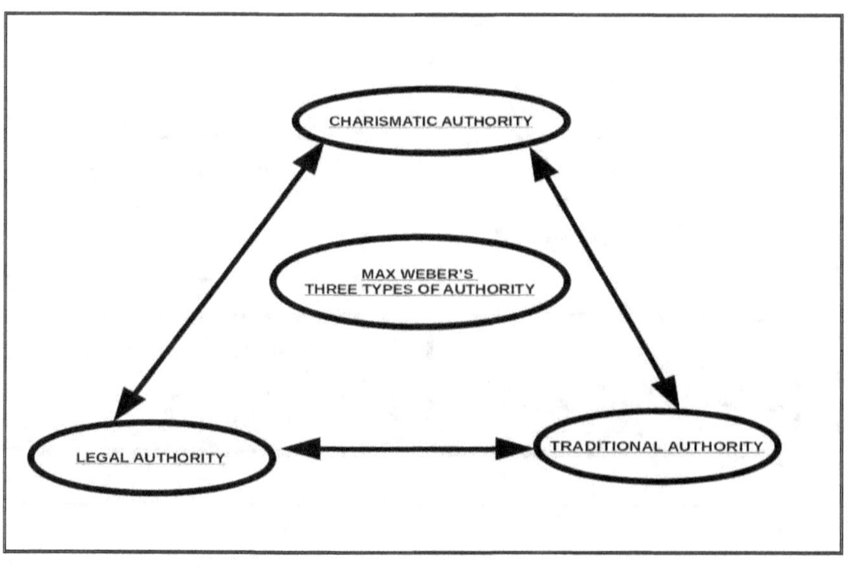

In Jammu and Kashmir during 1940's, traditional authority of Maharaja dynasty was on his last leg as a wave for democratize government was on rise all over the world .Charismatic authority is that authority which is derived from the leader's claims to a higher power or inspiration that is supported by his or her followers .

Sheikh Mohd. Abdullah was a charismatic personality in 1930's and he was very much influenced by Max's ideology. In Kashmir Valley, in 1930's the class system was like this. There were two groups - Capitalist class and Workers (like Marx's stratification).

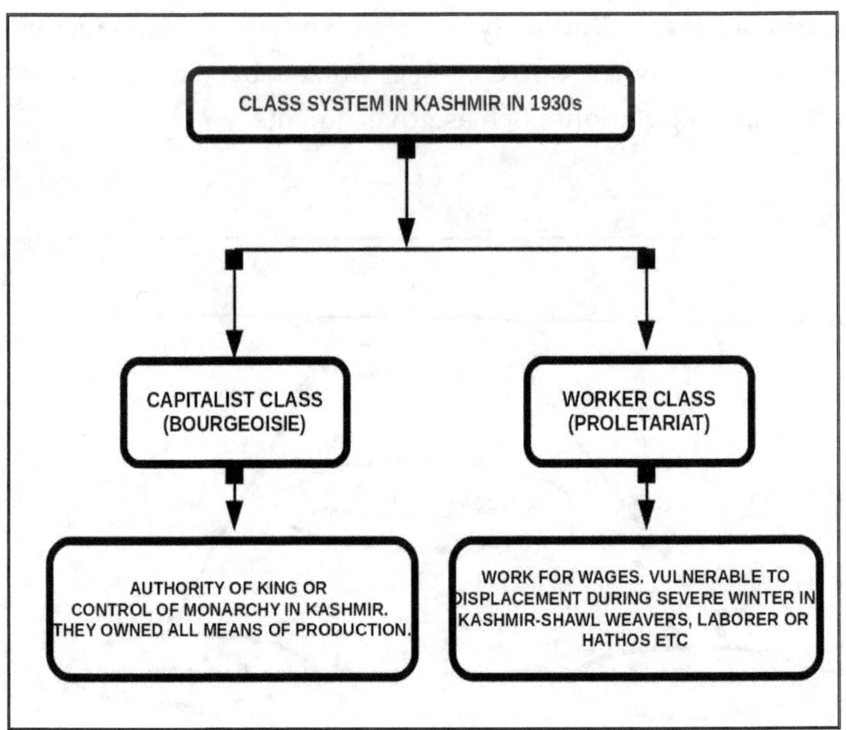

The economically poor Muslim class sees Sheikh Mohammad Abdullah as their leader against monarchy of Maharaja .For holding people at one common cause can be easily done with the use of religious ethnicity that is of being Muslims , oppressed by Infidels not by Monarchy ." I said too that national movements for freedom initially get their impetus from religion since religion is quick to arouse man's emotions. So, religion is the progenitor of national consciousness[49]". Sheikh Mohammad Abdullah," THE BLAZING CHINAR" An Autobiography.

Sheikh's Abdullah, an eminent educationist knew this as cited from his above quotes. The illiterate and poor society of 1930's Kashmir gave Abdullah a platform to unite the people against the autocratic rule of Maharaja. It is clear from above, 'Religious Ethnicity' is one of the important tools which can be utilized for political power.

The power full can shape society in accordance with their own interests and directs, the actions of others [Tumin, 1953]. When Sheikh Mohd Abdullah achieved this political power by using his charismatic authority (based on religious ethnicity) Choudhary Ghulam Abbas Khan (a leader of Jammu province) and Dogra Muslims (Chibhalis Region) get marginalized.

When Maharaja Hari Singh give Sheikh Mohd. Abdullah traditional political authority due to emergency conditions formed by the Pakistan 's Tribal invasion, Sheikh emerged as a popular or masses leader.

After the cease fire declaration, Dogra Muslim leadership got sidelined and Maharajah's traditional authority came to an end. Sheikh Mohammad Abdullah, after achieving traditional political authority along with charismatic

---

49 Abdullah, Sheikh Mohammad, The Blazing Chinar- an Autobiography, Srinagar, Gulshan Books Pg. 185.

authority, won the tug of war become the all in all authority of Jammu and Kashmir state in 1947 and after.

Choudhary Ghulam Abbas of Muslim conference was forced to exile in Pakistan and similarly Mirwaiz Maulvi Yusuf Shah leader of Muslim conference was forced to exile in POJK (Pakistan Occupied Jammu and Kashmir) after Sheikh Abdullah endorsed Maharaja Hari Singh's decision to accede to India.

A GREAT ETHNIC DIVIDE 1947

(JAMMU PROVINCE)

24th NOVEMBER 1947
BLACK NOVEMBER OF 1947 IN POJK

The tragedies of J&K constitute a long, horrific tale of Death & Inhumanity. It has many villains & no heroes.

- Dr. Ganesh Malhotra

J&K Strategic & Political Analyst.

CHAPTER 11: ETHNIC AND DEMOGRAPHIC GENOCIDE OF 1947

"To *recall those days of communal orgy my only objective is to point out that a communalist and killer has no religion. It was the humanity that was the victim of communal fanatics ......*
We should better learn appropriate lessons from history and not allow the communal fanatics of one or the other community to vitiate atmosphere and disturb communal pace and harmony"

Ved Basin who witnessed the Jammu massacre in 1947.

To quote a 10 Aug 1948 report published in the Times, London: - "237000 Muslim were systematically exterminated – unless they escaped to Pakistan along the border – by the forces of the Dogra state headed by the Maharaja in person and aided by Hindus and Sikhs. This happened in Oct 1947 five days before the Pathan invasion and nine days before the Maharaja's accession to India"

Many Muslim families lost their family members by middle of October when important Hindu and Muslim festival - Dussehra and Eid ul Juha coincided leading to perpetrators and victims gathering in large numbers. Hundreds of Muslims in Jammu, kathua, Reasi and Udampur were killed on Eid.

Among them was the prominent Jammu Muslim leader Chaudhry Ghulam Abbas's daughter who was abducted in

Nov 1947 and could not be traced for a long time. Then, in 1948 she was found in Punjab. The recovery of Chaudhry Abbas's daughter could be made possible with the intervention at the highest level between the government of India and Pakistan.

But thousand others consumed by the horrible history were not so lucky, among the unfortunate lot was the prominent Muslim leader Chaudhry Hamid Ullah khan `s daughter. She was killed during this massacre of 1947.

The fall of 1947, Jammu was no longer safer for Muslims but what really happened was spoken about by Mahatma Gandhi in the following words "the Hindus and Sikhs of Jammu, and those who had gone there from outside killed Muslims, the Maharaja of Kashmir is responsible for what is happening there.... A large no of Muslims has killed there and Muslims women have been dis-honored'. Muslims people assembled at various camp like khati khan Talab camp with the promise of being safely taken to Sialkot. But trucks after trucks that were supposed to take Muslims to Sialkot (Pakistan) came back with blood dripping from them.

In Nov 1947, The New York Times reported that Jammu had seen the scenes of massacre against Mohammedans in retaliation for Hindus and Sikhs deaths in west Punjab (Pakistan). "Watching officials and military officers directed a huge mob against the Muslims refugee convey (that) it hacked to pieces. Around 123 villages were completely de-populated". - the report stated[50].

Violence Against Hindus and Sikhs in Rajouri and Mirpur

The western district of Punch and Mirpur raised an armed rebellion in the first week of Oct 1947 which was joined by Pastun tribesmen from the NWFP (North west frontier province) and the adjoining princely states and tribal areas .The rebels took control of most of the country side of these district by the end of the month , driving the Hindus and the Sikhs from there to the towns where the states troops garrisoned . Then, starting 24 Oct, towns themselves fell to the rebels: Bimber (24 Oct), Rajouri (7 Nov), Mirpur and Deva and Vatala (25 Nov).

Their non-Muslims populations Hindus, scheduled caste, Sikhs etc. had to face "T**otal Annihilation**[51]" (Das Gupta 'Jammu and Kashmir 2012, page -97).

Rajouri: - According to the Indian sources, an estimated 30000 Hindus and Sikhs living in Rajouri were reportedly killed, wounded or abducted.

Mirpur Massacre: - Many Hindus and Sikhs, on and after 25 Nov 1947 gathered in Mirpur for shelter and protection were killed by the Pakistani troops and tribes' men. Estimated

---

50 Zaid Qazi, (05 Nov 2017), Jammu Massacre@70: Frenzy of Suraiya, and the silence of History. https://www.google.com/amps/freepressKashmir.com

51 Das, Gupta, 2012, Jammu & Kashmir Pg. 97.

measure of death count as over 20000. A greatly shocked Sardar Ibrahim painfully confirmed that Hindus were "**Disposed of**" in Mirpur in Nov 1947, although he does not mention any figure.

<u>TOTAL ESTIMATED CAUSALITIES (Hindus and Muslims)</u>

Muslims	20000 – 100000 persons
Hindus and Sikhs	20000- 30000 persons

<u>Estimated causalities during 1947 in Jammu and Kashmir from different sources[52].</u>

It is cleared from the above, whether displacement, killing had been occur during Oct -Nov 1947, it was in Jammu province. Jammu province was totally obliterated and nobody took responsibility and not even court of inquiry was established to assess the riot / massacre.

In Lahore (Pakistan's Punjab) it was a great irony that a court of inquiry was established to assess about the Ahar – Ahmedi riots in western Punjab Pakistan 1953 but no such court of inquiry took place in Jammu after the declaration of cease fire line about the Jammu massacre of 1947.

Thus, this was the total destruction of Jammu province Dogra – Muslim and Hindu ethic cultural unity. Consequently, Jammu province was divided into two parts – west Jammu (POJ) Pakistan Occupied Jammu and East

52 Dr Vaid SP, 2007, How Partition rocked Jammu & Kashmir, Jammu, Shyama Publications Pg. 53.

Jammu (Indian part) and Jammu province reduced to minority from majority in political landscape.

Consequent upon this, the legislative assembly of Jammu and Kashmir which was initially composed of 100 members, later increased to 111 by the constitution of Jammu and Kashmir Act of 1988. Out of these 111 seats ,24 seats are designated for the territorial constituencies of the state that were occupied by Pakistan in 1947.These seats remain officially vacant as per the section 48 of the state constitution. Hence ,87 seats remain the actual number while the magic figure remains 44 to form government. The Kashmir region has 46 seats, the Jammu region has 37 seats and the Ladakh region has 04 seats.

It means that due to POJK (Pakistan Occupied Jammu and Kashmir) the total loss to the state is of 24 seats which gives the Kashmiri Political Parties upper hand than Jammu province parties after 1947.Because these seats are almost part of Jammu province before the declaration of cease fire line. If these seats were with in Jammu provide, the Chief Minister will definitely from Jammu not from Kashmir valley.

CHAPTER 12: CONCEPT OF NIRDIYAI DHARTI

Concept of Nirdiyai land

"Nirdiyai" is a Hindi word, etymologically, it is a combination of two words i.e "**Nir**" and "**Diyai**".

Nir means 'no' and diyai means 'mercy' or in other words diyai means compassionate heart

Nir -diyai

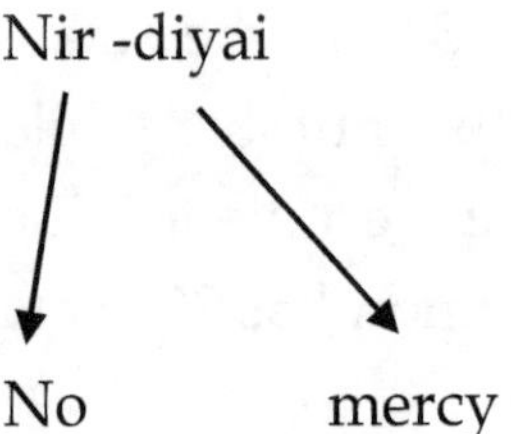

No mercy

Thus, it means land with no mercy.

Nir- diyai

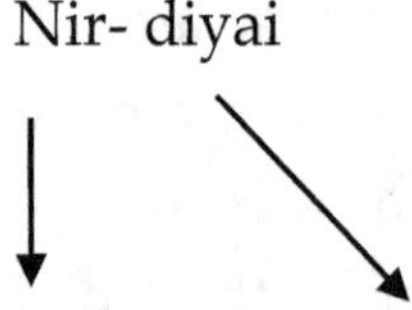

No compassionate heart

Thus, it means land with no compassionate heart.

I was told by my father that the land along the present IB (international border) / Loc (line of control) /working boundary of Pakistan in R S Pura sector is called Nirdiyai dharti. The drought like conditions prevails over in this area and food and water was scarce. And when people go into this land, they feel hungry and unrest full. He told me that this land is called Nirdiayi Dharti because it is associated with the "Epic story of Sharvan kumar". Sharvan Kumar was very unfortunates as both of his parents were blind. Sharvan Kumar was very dutiful son and did all the work for them. And when his parents desired to go on a pilgrimage, he created a balance like device where he could carry his parents on his shoulders and take them on pilgrimage. During their travel, they reached a forest and felt very thirsty and asked Sharvan to get some water in order to quench their thrust. Sharvan left his parents in the forest and went to river to bring water for them.The king of Ayodhya was King Dashrath and he was very good at hunting. He stepped into the forest with an attention to hunt. He had an innate quality of hunting as he could throw his arrow from miles if he could hear a sound. Hearing the sound, Dashrath mistook it as the sound of a deer drinking water. He aims his arrow from where the sound was coming and threw it. The arrow breezed through the air and pierced straight into the chest of Sharvan Kumar. He cried in pain and eventually fell on the ground. The moaning sound did not escape the ears of Dashrath. He reached the place immediately and saw the innocent boy crying out of unbearable pain. Dashrath noticed a vessel lying beside him and the boy was all covered with mud and blood. After seeing the sight, Dashrath become upset and cursed himself.

After hearing the news of son's death, Sharvan parents also died beside his son. However before dying they cursed king Dashrath for killing their innocent son. They said that as they could not tolerate their son's death and hence, they died, similarly King Dasharatha would also face the same consequences one day. He would also die due to his son's loss. This curse was found to be true because king Dashrath

could not bear the pain and died at the time when Lord Ram went on exile for fourteen long years.
Geographically this area is called is 'kalor' or saline type soil which is not so useful for agriculture. Mostly 'kai and 'sarkande' grow over there.

Local people often called this land as 'ujadh' or desolate land. In 1940's people used to grow maize, urdh (black lintels/ maa ki dal), cotton over this land. To deal with scarcity of food, people used to kill 'saiy' and wild boar. They put the pieces of **saiy** and wild boar in earthen pot after treating them with salt and turmeric and placed these earthen pots under the ground. They used these as pickle for dealing with food scarcity for their survival.

Today in 2019 even after the development of irrigation facilities and Green revolution the land still remain as NIrdiayi dharti. Because many fence living people died over this land along with defense personnel because of shelling and sniping by Pakistan. People lost their sons and are not able to sleep peacefully. The cattle get killed and crops get destroyed mercilessly. Thus, the Nirdiyai land can never be at peace.

CHAPTER 13: JAMMU - SAILKOT RAILWAY LINE CLOSED

The Jammu -Sialkot line was a 43 km (27 miles) broad guage[53] branch of the North Western Railway from Wazirabad junction, Punjab (Pakistan) to Jammu through Sialkot junction. The section from Sialkot to Jammu (tawi) was 27 miles (43 kms), partly lying in Punjab and partly in Jammu and Kashmir[54] .It was built in 1890 and was the first railway line in the state of Jammu and Kashmir. It was dismantled after the partition of India, with a replacement line built from Pathankot to Jammu.

The journey time between Sialkot and Jammu (tawi) averaged about 90 minutes. the intermediate stations listed in the timetable are (from west to east).

1. **Sialkot**
2. **Suchetgarh**
3. **Ranbirsingh pora**
4. **Miranshaib**
5. **Jammu Cantt.**

The India -Pakistan border crossed the line 0.26 miles (0.42 km) east of Suchetgarh station. Thus, the first station on the

53 Newman's Indian Bradshaw, February 1935, Newman & Co limited, Calcutta, 1935, Pg. 138.

54 History of Indian Railways, Corrected upto 31 March 1933, Government of India Press, 1934, Pg. 151, 159.

Indian side was Ranbir Singh Pura[55]. The line has been dismantled. The station building such as Ranbir Singh Pura and others are lying abandoned. The old (Jammu tawi) railway station at Vikram Chowk was demolished to make way for an Art center. No interest in the line has been expressed by archaeological authorities or by the Northern Railway division of India.

The remnants of Jammu- Sialkot rail link is gradually fading away in absence of any measures to preserve the remains of the oldest narrow-gauge track.

Before partition of the sub-continent it was the first ever train which had entered the state of Jammu and Kashmir. The subsequent government in the state have failed to preserve the remains of this historically, politically and emotionally important link to POJK (Pakistan occupied Jammu and Kashmir). People used this rail link to move freely between Jammu and Sialkot for trade and had stronger relations with Pakistan Punjab.

The R S Pura railway station and the railway line and its adjacent land for up to Jammu has been encroached by the people. The locality established on the railway line near erstwhile Ranbir Singh Pura railway station is called 'Patri'. Mostly the refugees hailing erstwhile Punch state (POJK) are now residing on the railway line (Patri)of Jammu- Sialkot

---

55 MBK Malik, 1962, Hundred years of Pakistan Railways, Karachi, Pakistan Pg. 204.

Railway line. The government not able to resettle them from this historical site[56].

According to Sheikh Mohammad Abdullah – "the people of Jammu province are culturally and linguistically akin to the neighboring Punjab and has always been under its influence. They are related to matrimony and commerce. Since there were Railway facilities up to Jammu, they would conveniently interact[57]." Before 1947, Lahore and Sialkot were central focus of politics and trade akin to New Delhi of today. Opening of this route ,can lead to interaction among people at international level and better relationship among the two neighbors (India and Pakistan).But other side of the coin is that it will lead to joining of Dogra Muslim Ethnic Community residing in the POJK(Pakistan occupied Jammu and Kashmir)with Dogra Hindu Ethnic Community (Indian Jammu and Kashmir). And no Kashmir based politician would like to do so because united Dogra Hindu-Muslim Ethnic Community will make the Kashmiri Ethnic Community a minority. Politically it will neutralize whatever Kashmiri Politicians had gained from the Jammu and Kashmir state since 1947 after the declaration of cease-fire line on 01 Jan. 1949.

---

56 Akshaya Azad, (March14, 2015) Historic Jammu- Sialkot Rail Line in Oblivion retrieved from https://www.greaterkashmir.com/news/more/news/historic-jammu-sialkotrailinoblivion.

57 Abdullah, Sheikh Mohammad, The Blazing Chinar- an Autobiography, Srinagar, Gulshan Books.

Old Railway station of RS Pura

CHAPTER 14: JAMMU AND KASHMIR AT PRESENT

IB - WORKING BOUNDARY OF PAKISTAN (A NEW FASHION - GAIN SYMPATHY OR VICTIM CARD)

A Normal Day, 19 Jan 2018

On 19th Jan 2018, heavy shelling was going on in R S Sector, I am wondering where is Kashmriyat, Insaniyat and Jamurit for our people. People are starting to move out of the shelling to safer place. More than sixty thousand people move out to safer places. When people blame in the social media and books for the brutality of military in Kashmir at the same time, the people along with Defense force personnel bears heavy firing of 81 mm Mortar and 82 mm Mortar, Light Machine Guns, Medium Machine Guns and Automatic Grenade Launchers.

Dogriat (Dogri folk): - A 19 yrs. old girl of Arnia named Neelam Devi D/o Sat Paul residence of Arnia had died a day before along with a Border Security Force solider by a splinter of Mortar shell.

A vegetable vendor is hawking outside but nobody wants any vegetable to cook food at this tense situation. An ambulance along with an army jeep is moving like a rocket to reach a government hospital where few doctors are trying their best to safe the injured arriving from the IB (international border)/ working boundary of Pakistan.

Government hospital RS Pura is full of patients who have been injured accompanied by their relatives. There is news that three more soldiers had martyred. Few buses are available on street as a result and daily commuters are looking helpless. Day-to-day opening of grocery shop is in confusion, some are open some are delayed. Fuel stations has been overcrowded by the people to get the petrol and diesel so that they can take their relatives out of villages along with IB / working boundary.

When I reach the Government Degree College in Ranbir Singh Pura, 5 km away from IB preparing for Bio-metric attendance everything is looking normal. The Principle of the college is busy in making official letter to honorable Minister of Legislative Assembly to get the land allotted for the expansion of the college.

Outside my room near the window few college girls are standing in sunshine as it is cold month of January. A girl is narrating horribly the situation she had seen in the government hospital where she had gone along with her uncle to see her injured classmate. She was narrating like this "many are injured so badly with bullets that they are shifted to Government Medical College, Bakshi Nagar. Three BSF soldiers had martyred because of bullet injury". She is telling it like she had seen some horror movie.

In the Staff room most of the staff which is coming from Jammu city to give their 'scholarly knowledge' to students are not bothered at all about shelling going on in the IB / working boundary of Pakistan. Some female staff members are discussing about their children birthday, Kashmiri shawl which one the staff members have bought at an expensive amount. I felt like an alien in between them.

One of the students came and told me that two more women had died by shelling at village Sai. Thereafter three more girls told me that at village korotana khurd two boys have died and many injured has been shifted to Government medical college Bakshi Nagar. One staff member from village Arnia shows the pictures of distorted humans in hospital and animals killed in shelling. Another staff member said, "they are also dying", they mean POJK (Pakistan occupied Jammu and Kashmir) / Azad Kashmir people.

One more staff member did not take part in this discussion as he feel that brutality in Kashmir is more than IB. This is how a day started in R S Pura town. All is seeming normal as from the last so many years shelling is part of our lives.

NEWS18 » INDIA

3-MIN READ

'Why Don't They Kill Us Once and For All': For LoC Residents, Life is a Perpetual State of War

Terrified villagers broke down on Saturday when government officials visited them. They were begging to be evacuated. The administration has made arrangements to shift some of them to a safer village.

Courtesy: News18.com

If you travel along these border villages you can see many statues has been built in the memory of martyred soldiers who has laid their lives for saving their country from militancy, shelling and wars like 1965, 1971, Kargil war etc. In the recent report on Jan 17 2018, daily excelsior published the news like this.

195 Security men martyred in Jammu and Kashmir terror attacks.

Jammu, Jan 17 Government today said that 195 security personnel have sacrificed their lives in the past three years in terrorist attacks in the state. In a written reply to the question of Bhartiya Janata Party member Ramesh Arora in the Upper house today, Minister in charge Home said that during last three years 195 security personnel have lost their lives in terror attack in the state. The Minister further added that 195 security personnel attained martyrdom in terrorist related incident and out of these 78 are martyred during 2017, 74 in 2016, while 43 during 2015.

Courtesy Daily Excelsior 18 Jan 2018.

These soldiers belong mostly to the farmer's family and poor farm laborers who live mostly near LOC or working boundary of Pakistan. These young soldiers, when they are children mostly at the age of 12 -14 years' work in farm and with great difficulty pass 10th or 12th class examination through Government school and after that join defense forces and lay down their life for the cause of nationalism.

As and when a rally happened for recruitment, you can see thousands of them around the recruitment centers. Sometimes they are also fooled by touts and agents in lieu of providing them job in defense.

These young students even do not know -
what is the meaning of POJK (Pakistan occupied Jammu and Kashmir)?
Where it lies geographically?

But they fight against terrorism, cross border firing, snipping, suicide attacks and stone palters also.
Sometimes the answer I got was that civil societies will keep all the things in place. But no civil societies came forward to solve the problem. In fact, no one is interested as we have no foreign funding.

<u>Three lakhs can't live in their own state</u>

Kashmiri pandit organization this year also, are going to observe, on Jan 19, what they call "the holocaust day "in the context of Kashmiri pandit migration on 19 Jan 1990 as the "exodus day".
Native Kashmiri pandit who claimed to be aboriginal inhabitants of Kashmir enter 29th year in exile.

Killing one and scaring a thousand was concentrated plan executed by the terrorists. Where is the state government at that time? Where are the civil societies? The forced migration shattered physically and psychologically the Kashmiri pandits migrants.

But it is the great bravery of this periphery living people that they work hard in farms when young and die for nation as soldiers but do not join as militants in spite of unemployment conditions. In fact, by sloganeering against Pakistan and taking banner before secretariat in Jammu and in Delhi will not solve their problem. What can they do?

They give you doses of their future plan for us. Our people will get doses and come back as it is happening since 1947. Their Utopian plan will not be implemented because they belong to different world of ideological differences which common man does not understand.

Who is killing whom?

This chain of killing each other has started from civilians living in Jammu and Kashmir and POJK. Mostly small farmers children's join defense forces or as militants, do their best and kill each other.

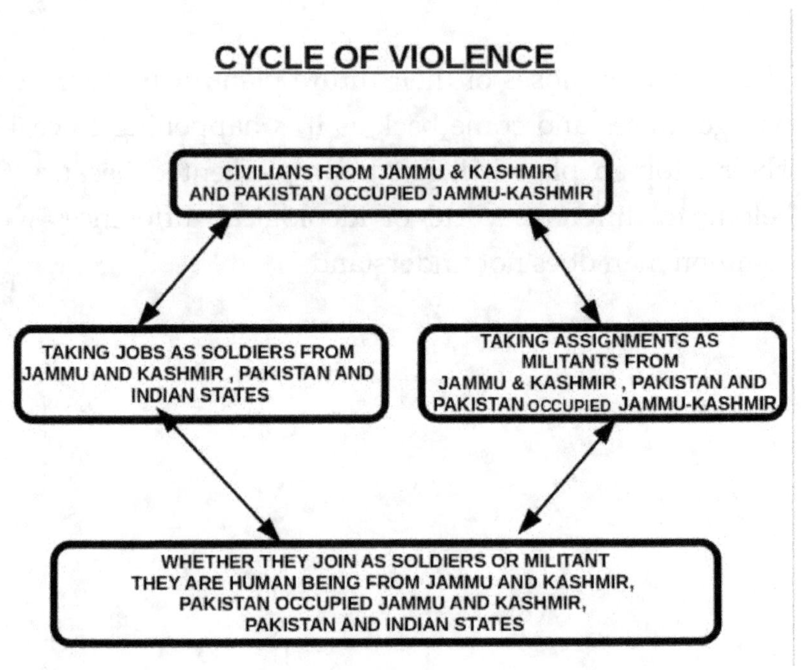

From kathua ➡ Jammu ➡ Uhampur ➡ Ramban Srinagar ➡ kargil, we can find multiple statues of soldiers and graveyards of militants are there. We kill each other by tagging each other as militants or soldiers.

What a civilized and democratize way of killing each other!

One Kashmiri politician says 'Kashmiri boys pelting stones is our children and separatist boys joining as militants are also our children's'. I agree with him. But my views are that the policemen, Army, BSF, CRPF boys are not our children. Why this step motherly attitude? If they (soldiers) are they mercenaries of India and separatist boys are not the mercenaries of Pakistan.

Today in Jammu and Kashmir, four things are part of life

1. Sniping at LOC / IB
2. Suicide Bombings and Militants Attack
3. Statues of martyred soldiers
4. Graveyards of militants

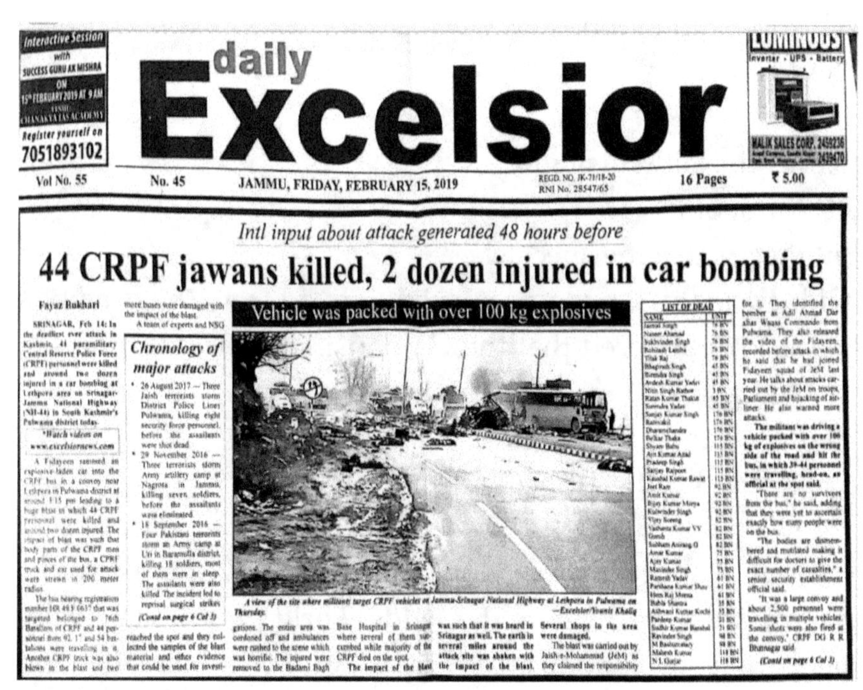

daily Excelsior

Vol No. 55 No. 45 JAMMU, FRIDAY, FEBRUARY 15, 2019 REGD. NO. JK-71/18-20 RNI No. 28547/65 16 Pages ₹ 5.00

Intl input about attack generated 48 hours before

44 CRPF jawans killed, 2 dozen injured in car bombing

Fayaz Bukhari

SRINAGAR, Feb 14: In the deadliest ever attack in Kashmir, 44 paramilitary Central Reserve Police Force (CRPF) personnel were killed and around two dozen injured in a car bombing at Lethpora area on Srinagar-Jammu National Highway (NH-44) in South Kashmir's Pulwama district today.

**Watch videos on www.excelsiornews.com*

A Fidayeen rammed an explosive-laden car into the CRPF bus in a convoy near Lethpora in Pulwama district at around 3.15 pm leading to a huge blast in which 44 CRPF personnel were killed and around two dozen injured. The impact of blast was such that body parts of the CRPF men and pieces of the bus, a CRPF truck and car used for attack were strewn in 200 meter radius.

The bus bearing registration number HR 49 F [illegible] that was targeted belonged to 76th Battalion of CRPF and 44 personnel from [illegible] battalions were travelling in it. Another CRPF truck was also blown in the blast and two more buses were damaged with the impact of the blast.

A team of experts and NSG reached the spot and they collected the samples of the blast material and other evidence that could be used for investigations. The entire area was cordoned off and ambulances were rushed to the scene which was horrific. The injured were removed to the Badami Bagh Base Hospital in Srinagar where several of them succumbed while majority of the CRPF died on the spot.

The impact of the blast was such that it was heard in Srinagar as well. The earth in several miles around the attack site was shaken with the impact of the blast. Several shops in the area were damaged.

The blast was carried out by Jaish-e-Mohammad (JeM) as they claimed the responsibility for it. They identified the bomber as Adil Ahmad Dar alias Waqas Commando from Pulwama. They also released the video of the Fidayeen, recorded before attack in which he said that he had joined Fidayeen squad of JeM last year. He talks about attacks carried out by the JeM on troops, Parliament and hijacking of airliner. He also warned more attacks.

The militant was driving a vehicle packed with over 100 kg of explosives on the wrong side of the road and hit the bus, in which 39-44 personnel were travelling, head-on, an official at the spot said.

"There are no survivors from the bus," he said, adding that they were yet to ascertain exactly how many people were on the bus.

"The bodies are dismembered and mutilated making it difficult for doctors to give the exact number of casualties," a senior security establishment official said.

"It was a large convoy and about 2,500 personnel were travelling in multiple vehicles. Some shots were also fired at the convoy," CRPF DG R R Bhatnagar said.

(Contd on page 6 Col 3)

Chronology of major attacks

- 26 August 2017 — Three Jaish terrorists storm District Police Lines Pulwama, killing eight security force personnel, before the assailants were shot dead.
- 29 November 2016 — Three terrorists storm Army artillery camp at Nagrota in Jammu, killing seven soldiers, before the assailants were eliminated.
- 18 September 2016 — Four Pakistani terrorists storm an Army camp at Uri in Baramulla district, killing 18 soldiers, most of them were in sleep. The assailants were also killed. The incident led to reprisal surgical strikes.

(Contd on page 6 Col 3)

Vehicle was packed with over 100 kg explosives

A view of the site where militants target CRPF vehicles on Jammu-Srinagar National Highway at Lethpora in Pulwama on Thursday. —Excelsior/Younis Khaliq

LIST OF DEAD

NAME	UNIT
Jaimal Singh	76 BN
Naseer Ahmad	76 BN
Sukhvinder Singh	76 BN
Rohitash Lamba	76 BN
Tilak Raj	76 BN
Bhagirath Singh	45 BN
Birendra Singh	45 BN
Avdesh Kumar Yadav	45 BN
Nitin Singh Rathor	3 BN
Ratan Kumar Thakur	45 BN
Surendra Yadav	45 BN
Sanjay Kumar Singh	176 BN
Ramvakil	176 BN
Dharamchandra	176 BN
Belkar Thaka	176 BN
Shyam Babu	115 BN
Ajit Kumar Azad	115 BN
Pradeep Singh	115 BN
Sanjay Rajput	115 BN
Kaushal Kumar Rawat	115 BN
Jeet Ram	92 BN
Amit Kumar	92 BN
Bijay Kumar Morya	92 BN
Kulwinder Singh	92 BN
Vijay Soreng	82 BN
Vasantha Kumar VV	82 BN
Gursh	82 BN
Subham Aniruag G	82 BN
Amar Kumar	75 BN
Ajay Kumar	75 BN
Maninder Singh	75 BN
Ramesh Yadav	61 BN
Parthana Kumar Shaw	61 BN
Hem Raj Meena	61 BN
Babla Shantra	35 BN
Ashwani Kumar Kochi	35 BN
Pardeep Kumar	21 BN
Sudhir Kumar Banshal	21 BN
Ravinder Singh	98 BN
M Basumatary	98 BN
Mahesh Kumar	118 BN
N L Gurjar	118 BN

Courtesy Daily Excelsior

2 Army officers killed in Pak sniping in Kupwara

Excelsior Correspondent

SRINAGAR Dec 21: Two Army officers were killed in sniping by Pakistani troops along the Line of Control in North Kashmir's Kupwara district this afternoon.

A senior Army officer said that Pakistani troops in violation of ceasefire opened the sniper fire upon the Army's 2/8 GR posts in Peer Baba Grahat Post along the LoC in Jumgund area of Kupwara district.

Two Army officers suffered serious injuries in the attack and were immediately evacuated to military hospital Drugmulla where one of them, Junior Commissioned Officer (JCO) Subedar Gamar Thapa, 42, succumbed to injuries.

The other injured, Junior Commissioned Officer Subedar Raman Thapa was later referred to Army's 92 base hospital Badamibagh Srinagar for advanced treatment. However, he succumbed to injuries in the hospital.

A senior police officer said that Army deployed along the LoC responded to the Pakistani fire, triggering the cross-border shelling in the area which was intermittently going on till this evening.

In the meantime, police today said Lashkar-e-Toiba (LeT) militant Zubair Shabir Bhat, who was arrested in Ganderbal district yesterday had come to Kangan with the intention to loot weapons from the security forces. "We managed to catch him and recovered a grenade from his possession", said SSP Ganderbal, Khalid Ahmed Poshwal.

"We have verified his category, we have also identified other local links and will take action against them also and will further investigate the matter. FIR has been registered against him in the Kangan Police Station which is still under investigation", he said.

"On getting the first hand information from the Srinagar Police about his movement in the area, we further looked into it while the militant was riding on scooty towards Kangan area of Ganderbal. We immediately informed the CRPF and cordoned off the area leading to the

(Contd on page 6 Col 3)

Courtesy Daily Excelsior

Excerpt from Ved Rahi's Dogri peom 'Jammu'

Why don't you send
The Army
Back to Delhi?
Extract the Giddadsinghi
Of 'Autonomy'
But then watch the spectacle!

(Giddadsinghi, is a magic portion derived from the head of a Jackal. It is believed that the Giddadsinghi enables a person to achieve anything that he desires).

Apathy and Indifference

The self-possessed successionist of the valley may play the victimization card before the wide world , but it is actually the people of Jammu who have suffered ,directly and indirectly , because of shenanigans of the ' karakul caps' (the poets allusion to the Kashmiri leaders who shows fondness for this headgear) and the violence sponsored by the neighboring country. Kashmir has hogged the limelight, casting a deep shadow on Jammu. In their own land, the people of Jammu have become second class citizens irrespective of their religion.

Courtesy – daily excelsior, Jammu Sunday march 17 2019.

CHAPTER 15: WHO'S WORLD IS THIS?

While writing this book a thought which continuously run in the back of mind is that who's world is this? why other decide who will live and who will not and how one should live. How can just by being charismatic leader and sitting at top position gives every right to one to decide the future of other. People often says no one enjoy absolute power in democracy but if this the case then how can every wrong happening all around got unnoticed. Why politicians do all the things for his own political needs expect the one which he or she entailed to do and ignore the masses. The one sitting at the top is ruining the life of millions under him but no one questions him .... Why? The answer is simple the Age gap. How can a person born in 60's will know the priorities of today's generation? A person of Analog age is deciding the age of digital age. Today the style, thought, thinking of 10-year kids is somehow far better than older generations. Here I want to clear that I am not against the Politicians but I want to highlight their priorities which is not the masses but power. At the end, they know that who's decision will prevail. Merely by putting maximum numbers of years in Politics should not be criteria of deciding the present and future of other.

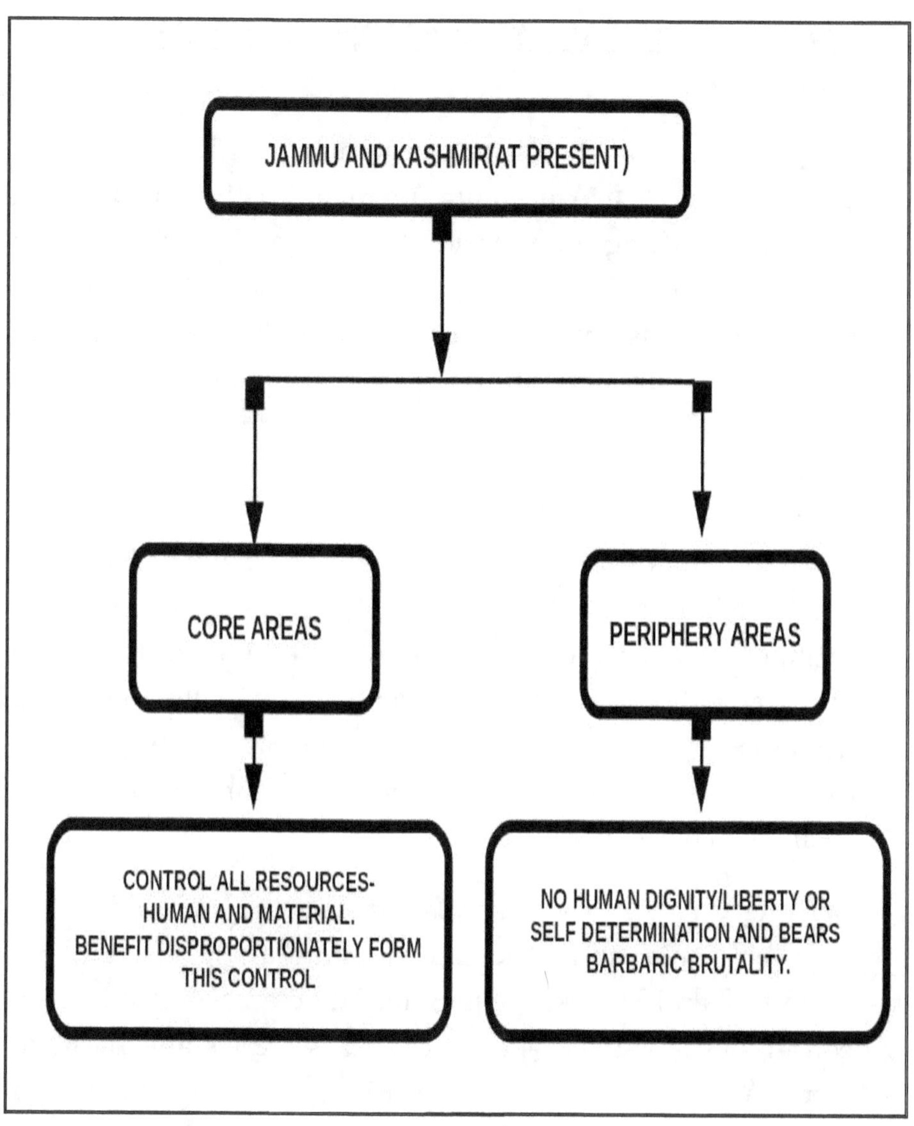
JAMMU AND KASHMIR(AT PRESENT)
CORE AREAS
PERIPHERY AREAS
CONTROL ALL RESOURCES-
HUMAN AND MATERIAL.
BENEFIT DISPROPORTIONATELY FORM
THIS CONTROL
NO HUMAN DIGNITY/LIBERTY OR
SELF DETERMINATION AND BEARS
BARBARIC BRUTALITY.

CORE-PERIPHERY ESCALATION IN JAMMU AND KASHMIR

Core Areas: In the context of Jammu and Kashmir, Core areas means 'The Area lying average 3-5 Kms away from LOC/IB/working Boundary of India and Pakistan. The people living in this area are not affected by shelling/sniping but militant attacks and suicide bombing incidents occur here. But the females and children are virtually not affected directly as like women and children residing near to the dividing line between India and Pakistan. They control all resources (Human/Material) and benefited dis-proportionality from this control. They are privileged to have easy access to all basic and advance facilities including educational institutes, medical services and recreational avenues. They are usually behaving immune to the reality on the ground and only react in extreme cases where the incident or event directly affect them, which is generally a rarity.

Periphery Areas: These are the areas along the diving line between India and Pakistan running along IB/working boundary and LOC subsequently. These areas are subject to continuous shelling of heavy caliber weapons and frequent sniper activities on both sides resulting in damage to life and property on daily basis. Further, these border dwellers have suffered from the numerous unaccounted mines laid in these areas over the last 75 years. Militancy and cross border action by opposing forces have made the life of people especially women and children stressful and miserable. On the development front, these areas represent a painful example of neglect socially and economically on the both sides of the border. The psychological stress due to insecurity of life and property have an overall long-term effect on the people of these regions. With nearly no human dignity/ Liberty/ self-determination, the people of these region find no end to this systematic barbaric brutality of egoistic political and religious clash.

I always try to answer this philosophical question that whole world is this? And periphery areas of Jammu and Kashmir belongs to which world. The apathy and indifference towards them will ever come to an end.

www.ingramcontent.com/pod-product-compliance
Lightning Source LLC
LaVergne TN
LVHW010112170826
845678LV00012B/2359
* 9 7 8 9 3 8 9 3 5 5 1 0 9 *